B R A D   P I T T

By THE EDITORS OF US   Designed by RICHARD BAKER   Photographs by MARK SELIGER

Introduction by CHRIS MUNDY

LITTLE, BROWN AND COMPANY   BOSTON   NEW YORK   TORONTO   LONDON

A Rolling Stone Press Book

EDITOR Holly George-Warren
ASSOCIATE EDITOR Shawn Dahl
EDITORIAL ASSISTANT Ann Abel
EDITORIAL CONTRIBUTORS
Lorraine Ali, Chris Mundy,
Barbara O'Dair, Peter Travers

DESIGNER Richard Baker
DESIGN CONSULTANT Fred Woodward
PHOTO EDITOR Fiona McDonagh
DESIGN ASSISTANTS Yoomi Chong,
Jennifer Chun, Bess Wong

First Edition

ISBN 0-316-89360-9

Library of Congress Catalog
Card Number 97-72965

10 9 8 7 6 5 4 3 2 1

RRD

Published simultaneously in Canada
by Little, Brown and Company (Canada) Limited

Printed in the United States of America

C ALLING BRAD PITT THE GOLDEN BOY OF the end of the Twentieth Century sounds a bit, well, over the top. But, honest to God, Pitt *is* the closest thing we've got to a storybook hero: he of the solid stock, killer smile, quiet ambition and consummate light touch, all of which translate quite neatly into box-office magic. He's a matinee idol straight out of the movies. • Pitt is the rebel with a homebody heart, a tantalizing meld of devil and angel, an altar boy in a ripped T-shirt, with a wicked grin. He's humble, even self-deprecatory, as if a belief in his limits is his best survival tool. Now that we see those limitations as less significant than anyone may have once cared to think, his humility is merely charming and convincing if not irritatingly beside the point. • From Pitt's first frisk in *Thelma & Louise* to his latest foray into the life of the Dalai Lama, he has moved with a kind of brilliant and steady confidence that puts some critics in mind of the young Robert Redford. But he's also got the down-home cred that the patrician Redford never has: Pitt's the dude with the disarming drawl. The hot male Hollywood actors who are his generational contemporaries – Tom Cruise, Johnny Depp, Sean Penn – each have their powers. Pitt has some of what each has got, and more: Even though he's their age, he seems new. So while he's lumped with Keanu Reeves and Leonardo DiCaprio and newcomers Skeet Ulrich and Matthew McConaughey, he has some life experience on which to draw. • Brad Pitt sits on the cusp of a new era in Hollywood, when a seismic shift in the pecking order has occurred. This was best illustrated, perhaps, in the drama from within the production of *The Devil's Own,* when the studio's brilliant casting coup to team Pitt with megastar Harrison Ford resulted in Pitt's eclipsing performance and some sore feelings. One thing you can bet on: Brad Pitt will probably get even better with age. • I'd like to think *US* magazine has done so itself. Pitt was our cover story in October 1995, an issue that marked a new age for the magazine – not incidentally, one that includes the talents of *US* art director Richard Baker, chief photographer Mark Seliger and contributing editor Chris Mundy. We've grown alongside Brad Pitt to the extent that, two years later, we present to you this book. ▫

BRAD
Lands

{ By Chris Mundy }

Looking back,
it was like trying to assess a flood's damage when, in reality, the rain had only begun to trickle. You want to be prepared, to sift through everything *before* the water is all around, yet you know it's impossible to actually sort anything out until the storm has unleashed its power, moved on and settled over someone else's life. And by that time, it's too late anyway.

That is how it was as I sat by the pool at Brad Pitt's new home in the Hollywood Hills in the late summer of 1994. Everything was still, but it was not a stillness to be trusted. Pitt had just finished filming *Interview With the Vampire* and *Legends of the Fall,* but neither had been released. And so we sat discussing the type of superstardom both of us believed was coming but had not yet arrived. We talked late into the night – about what responsibility might come with that stardom, how to build a career with longevity and legitimacy, and how to maintain privacy when one's name and face are public domain – all the while knowing that these were questions that couldn't be fully grasped until the moment was at hand.

There were, of course, signs that the storm would be no small matter. Offers were pouring in, and Pitt's going movie rate had leapt to more than $3 million per film on the strength of the forecast alone. Thinking back to my questions and his answers, though, what seems most apparent is that we both underestimated what was coming.

In many ways the house itself was the perfect metaphor for Pitt's state of limbo. A stunning old dwelling that rests within a beautifully sculpted compound, the home was practically empty. Boxes were scattered throughout the downstairs, and Pitt's three dogs were still at his old residence, being baby-sat by a friend. That night, Brad Pitt didn't live in the old, rented house of an up-and-coming actor, but he still wasn't prepared to live in the newly purchased Hollywood Hills mansion of a movie star.

He stood up from a poolside table to walk back indoors and stopped for a moment, staring at a spot that would soon be home to more pet iguanas than any grown man should rightfully own. "I mean, some things get harder, but then again, look at this place," he said, pointing across the sprawling backyard. "Things get much easier, too." He paused. "I'd love to have a [character actor] Wilford Brimley career – Wilford it straight down the pipe. That would be ideal. But who knows? It could all go away. I could pull a

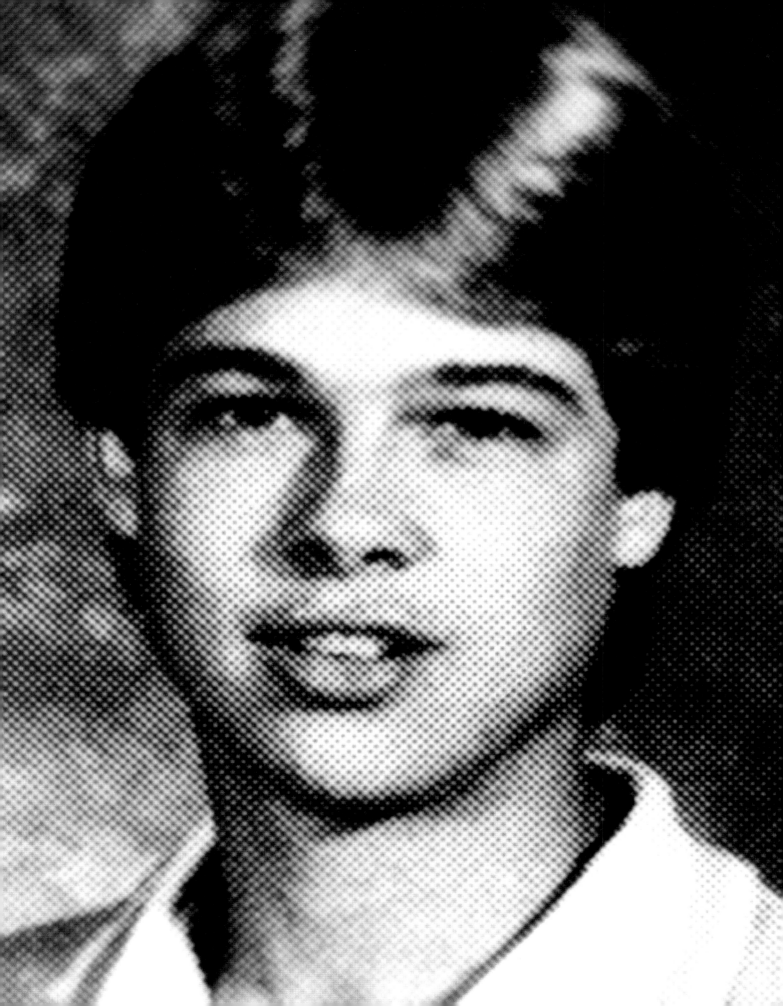

Mark Hamill." He stopped again. "You come here with this impression that just isn't true," he said finally. "Being in the movies doesn't make you laugh any harder and doesn't make you any less sad."

Pitt shuffled inside, and as the night dragged on he idly picked through boxes and ducked questions. Both of us were used to the routine. This night was the last formal interview in a process that had been going on for close to a year, and by this time the only thing that could have surprised me would have been if Pitt was *not* evasive. In the article that finally ran in *Rolling Stone,* I described him as "a cagey bastard – a good ol' boy with brains," and it is to his credit that though this statement holds true, he remains one of the most likable people I have ever interviewed.

"The truth is, I don't want people to know me," he said back then. "I don't know a thing about my favorite actors. Then they become personalities."

What Pitt failed to mention was that his methods of remaining aloof actually included hiding. The first attempt at a meeting took place in New Orleans during the filming of *Interview With the Vampire,* but when my plane touched down, Pitt took off. Finally, months later, during the final stages of filming *Interview,* Pitt and I met in London. The movie was being shot in Paris, but Pitt needed a break. He had two tickets bound for Scotland, and the friend he planned to go with had gotten sick. We went out the night before in London, met up the next morning and boarded a train to Scotland where, over the next three days, I discovered that traveling with Brad Pitt is great fun and interviewing him is a pain in the ass.

"I love to run around and have adventures," he said early in the trip. "Why do an interview? Why can't you just write about our adventures?"

So began the cat-and-mouse interrogation that eventually ended with that night in Los Angeles and one final meeting in New York. The Los Angeles interview was by far the most productive. At home Pitt was in a different gear than he had been while traveling, more at ease and willing to consider the questions being tossed his way. He claimed to be an explorer on the road and a hermit at home and, true to his word, in Los Angeles he was centered. That night Pitt explained his strange combination of needing to be either sequestered or on the lam.

"In L.A. the conversations don't vary much," said Pitt. "It's easy to disappear if you want to. Truth is, I've got other things I want to do, so I go do them. People take this all so seriously. My answer to everything I don't have an answer for is, 'Don't take everything so seriously.' Really. Lighten up, please. That's the way I do these movies. I do a few of these, I can do some other things. Because I have other things I'd really like to do that have nothing to do with movies."

I asked him if he ever worried that the nature of acting was inherently dishonest, if he sometimes felt like a professional liar.

"I'm not worried, because I'll never be too good an actor," he said. "I'm a good actor, I'm consistent, but I'll never be a great actor. Every now and then I'll be great. Every now and then I'll be lousy."

It's interesting to note that Pitt would amend that statement just over two years later, in another *Rolling Stone* interview. Times change quickly, especially in the high-stakes world of professional make-believe. If we were to sit by that same pool today, less than three years after that night, we would speak about Pitt's Oscar nomination for *12 Monkeys* and the fact that his asking price per film is now $17.5 million; and we would stare out on an estate that now encompasses two adjacent properties he has recently purchased – an estate he has shared with a fiancée, Gwyneth Paltrow, but where, at least for now, he lives alone.

But that is getting ahead of ourselves.

I always knew I'd leave Missouri. But it's like that Tom Waits song: 'I never saw the morning until I stayed up all night/I never saw my hometown until I stayed away too long.' I just wanted to see more. You'd come across a book or something on TV, and you'd see all these other worlds. It blew me away.

– Brad Pitt, 1994

When Brad Pitt finally left Missouri, in 1986, it was heading West, chasing the sunset all the way to California in a Nissan he had named Runaround Sue. He was twenty-two years old – two weeks and two credits shy of graduating from the University of Missouri with a degree in journalism. He claimed to be lighting out for the Art Center College of Design in Pasadena, but when he came clean nine months later and told his parents that he had landed an acting job, his father said simply, "Yeah, I thought so."

Early in his life, Pitt's father, Bill, had given him a piece of advice that had obviously resonated. While in a tennis tournament, Pitt had been screaming and throwing his racket. In our interview, Pitt remembered his father walking onto the court between games.

"He just said, 'Are you having fun?' " said Pitt. "I got all huffy and said no. He looked at me and said, 'Then don't do it,' and then walked away. Boy, that put me in my place. I should have gotten my ass kicked, but he was so above that."

More recently, in a 1995 *US* magazine interview, Pitt gave another insight into his father. "The other day I was on the phone with him," said Pitt. "And he goes: 'What's wrong with you? What's wrong?' And I said, 'Ah, you know. Just crap piling up.' And he goes, 'Well, you picked a crap job.' " Pitt laughed. "I liked that."

Talk to Brad Pitt for even the shortest time and he is bound to mention his parents. He calls them "the biggest guides in my life," says that his mother, Jane, was the first person to think he was talented ("she just thought it from day one," he says) and, along with his brother, Doug, thirty-one, and sister, Julie, twenty-eight, they make up a family that, by all accounts, is incredibly close-knit.

"Brad looks like his father and has the personality of his mother," Chris Schudy, one of Pitt's closest college friends, told me in 1994. "His mother is so down-to-earth, just a super woman. His dad is a great guy but more reserved. *A River Runs Through It* is almost a mirror image of Brad's family. When I saw the movie, I called him and said, 'You're not even acting. It's just your home unit minus Julie.' "

For William Bradley Pitt, the home unit first began on December 18, 1963, in the small town of Shawnee, Oklahoma. It quickly changed to Springfield, Missouri, the slightly larger Ozarks town where his parents moved when Bill, a manager for a trucking company (Jane was a high school counselor), got a better-paying trucking job. They and Pitt's siblings still reside there. Bill was often on the road, frequently with his kids along for the ride, since he figured the best way to keep a family close was ensuring it was together.

"I always looked up to both my brothers," said Julie. "I just thought they were the greatest things that ever happened. Doug and Brad really play off each other. We just had such a close family, and that gave us confidence. I think that's what allowed Brad to try to be an actor. Sometimes I can't believe that this guy from Springfield made it, but Brad has always succeeded in what he's done, and he's always had a way with people."

Pitt remembers the brotherly love as more brotherly, less loving. "I always had these dreams growing up," he told *Details* in 1992. "I'd wake up in a sweat crying my head off and it was always because something had happened to my brother. But I used to terrorize the kid. I'd lock him outside naked. I'd make him go get things and I'd *time* him. I'd say, 'If you can make it by twenty . . .' And then, just as he was running down the stairs, I'd say, 'Twenty-*one*. Aw, too bad. I woulda given you a prize.' "

Competition in the family room led to Pitt applying his skills at Kickapoo High School – he played team sports and participated in student government and the debate team – but he was just as likely to be suspended as on the honor roll.

"A lot of school is what you can get away with," he told *Rolling Stone*'s Jancee Dunn. "I threw a book at a teacher once. Not directly at. I didn't throw it hard, but it was a big book. It was one of the few times I was actually not doing anything wrong – she got on me in class and I started saying 'I didn't do anything.' And it was the old 'stop or I'm going to send you to the principal's office.' I said something like 'Fine, I'm going myself.' I tossed my book at her. I went to the principal's office. But I smashed her favorite coffee cup. I felt kinda bad. It was handmade."

Clearly, Pitt was restless in a town where the primary entertainment was the drive-in theater. "I was like an insider," he told *US* magazine in 1991, "inside of everything, like the cool stuff at school – but always looking *out*. Because it wasn't quite enough." And so he left, traveling 150 miles to the University of Missouri in Columbia, where he had two epiphanies, one major, one minor. The first was that he no longer felt a tie to the strict religious upbringing

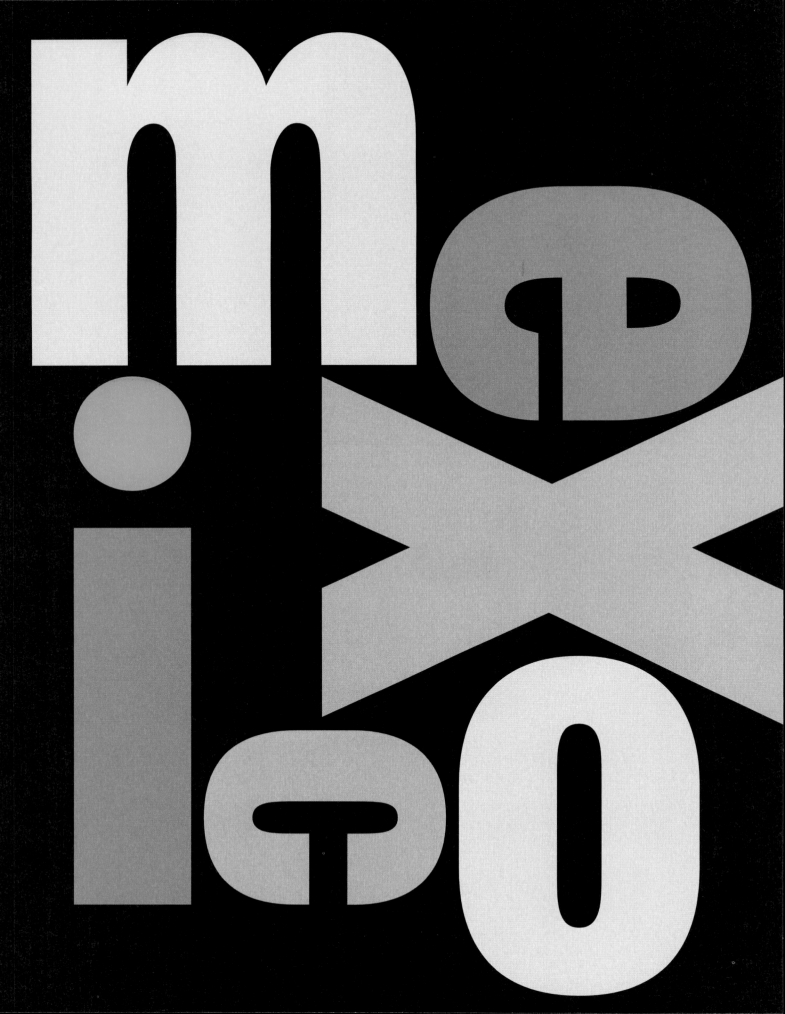

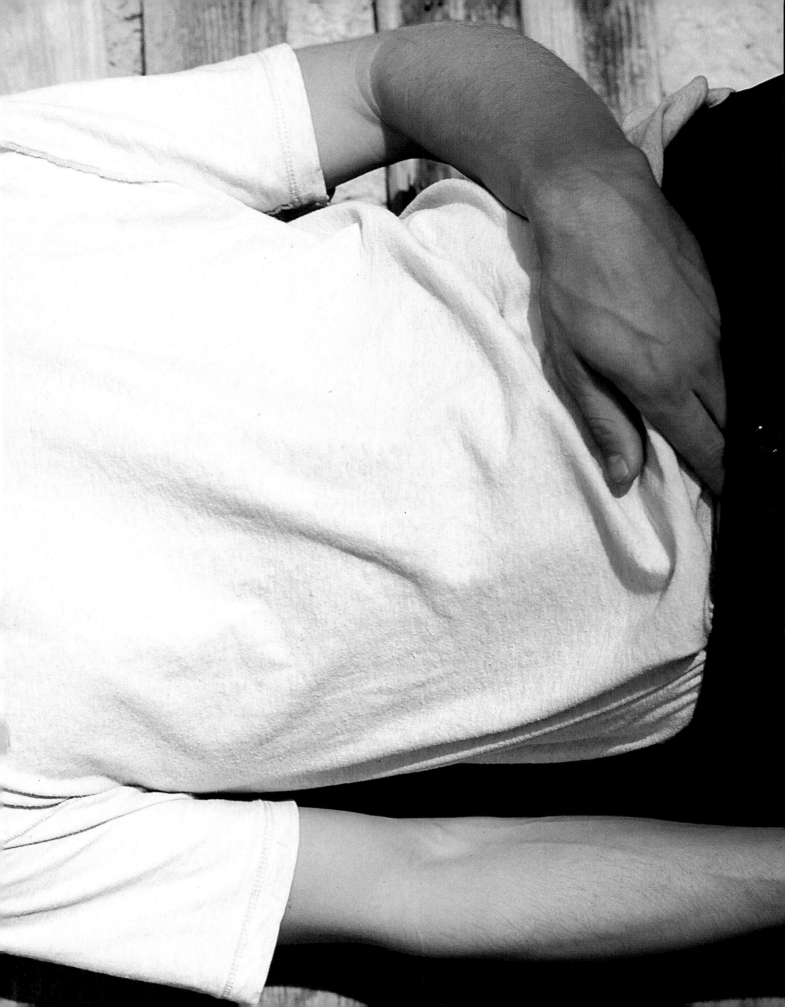

I MAY NOT KNOW EXACTLY WHERE THE NEED TO PERFORM COMES FROM AND I DON'T TOTALLY UNDERSTAND THE THRILL OF IT YET. BUT LET ME TELL YOU IT'S A REAL HIGH

(initially Baptist, then nondenominational) that had guided his life up to that point.

"I remember one of the most pivotal moments I've had was when I finally couldn't buy the religion I grew up with," said Pitt. "That was a big deal. It was a relief in a way that I didn't have to believe that anymore, but then I felt alone. It was this thing I was dependent on."

The second, less life-altering, insight to become clear was that, for Pitt, college was no place for clarity. He joined the fraternity Sigma Chi (where he acted a little in the frat's "Spring Fling" shows) and he minored in advertising, with the vague notion that he might do graphic design for an ad firm, but Pitt mostly concentrated on not concentrating. "It was incredible to just get away from home, living with a bunch of guys," he said in '94. "That school kind of revolves around a keg. We had this idea of *Animal House,* and there was definitely that aspect. It was a highlight, without a doubt. Then – like everything – you grow out of it."

And so Pitt left.

"You don't really get it into your head that you can leave, because – I don't know – not too many people leave," Pitt told *Rolling Stone* in 1992. "It was about time to graduate, and it just dawned on me: I can leave. It would be so simple, so easy. You load up the car, you point it west, and you leave. And everything's open."

The next thing Pitt knew, he and Runaround Sue hit the Pacific Coast with only a tank of gas and $325 to their names. Pitt had never been west of Wichita, Kansas, and had virtually no acting experience.

"It was such a relief," Pitt told me in '94. "I was coming to the end of college and the end of my degree and the beginning of my chosen occupation. I knew I didn't want to do it. I remember being so excited as I passed each state line. I drove in through Burbank, and the smog was so thick that it seemed like fog. I pulled in and went to McDonald's, and that was it. I just thought, *Shouldn't there be a little more?*"

To give away the Hollywood ending, there was.

{ UNEARTHING BRAD PITT }

Brad Pitt has taught himself many things (acting springs to mind), but perhaps his greatest gift is one Pitt was born with: his innate ability to shut out the rest of the world and wander aimlessly. In order to do this he must first disappear, of course – no easy feat – but a quick check of the data reveals that he has this part of the process down pat. In my 1994 article I wrote: "The significance . . . is that Pitt has been unearthed at all. . . . Just finding him is the hard part." The introduction of a 1995 *US* magazine Q&A included the words "Our first meeting was different, if only because Pitt was hard to find." And, finally, the first ten words of *Rolling Stone*'s most recent interview with Pitt, in 1997, are simply "Getting to Brad Pitt is a pain in the ass." *Amen.*

Some of this can be put down to Pitt's fear of interviewer intimacy, but much of it is, in reality, an innate personality trait. As Jane Pitt told *Rolling Stone* in 1992, "He's just someone who's always liked to try new things."

It doesn't always go over well. Pitt's friends are often angry because he's continually "drifting," a trait typified by something he explained in our interview. When filming a movie, Pitt makes a practice of purchasing a bicycle so he can steal away without attracting attention. Once production is finished, he simply locks up the bike and meanders on to the next locale. If he ever happens back to the film's location, the first thing Pitt does is search to see if the bike is still available. "I just like going for a little road trip," he explained. "I'm not leaving anywhere. I'm going somewhere."

The one constant during Pitt's intercontinental drifts is the sketchbook he scribbles in endlessly. Although he professes a great love of music – he collects guitars and friends such as Melissa Etheridge but insists his main connection is as a listener – architecture is Pitt's first love, and when he travels, his ideas flow continually from brain to paper. During our Scotland adventure, in fact, Pitt spent his days in Edinburgh and Glasgow tracking down the work of Charles Rennie Mackintosh, Scotland's answer to Frank Lloyd Wright and Pitt's answer to the question of who he lists as a hero. He freely admits he should have majored in architecture at Missouri, but – keeping in mind that this is a man who named his car around that time – he also admits to being much more enamored of the college lifestyle than the college course load.

"School was about getting out of classes instead of learning," Pitt told *Rolling Stone* in 1997. "And the architectural school was tough! They were studying day and night! I mean, I was in college, man!"

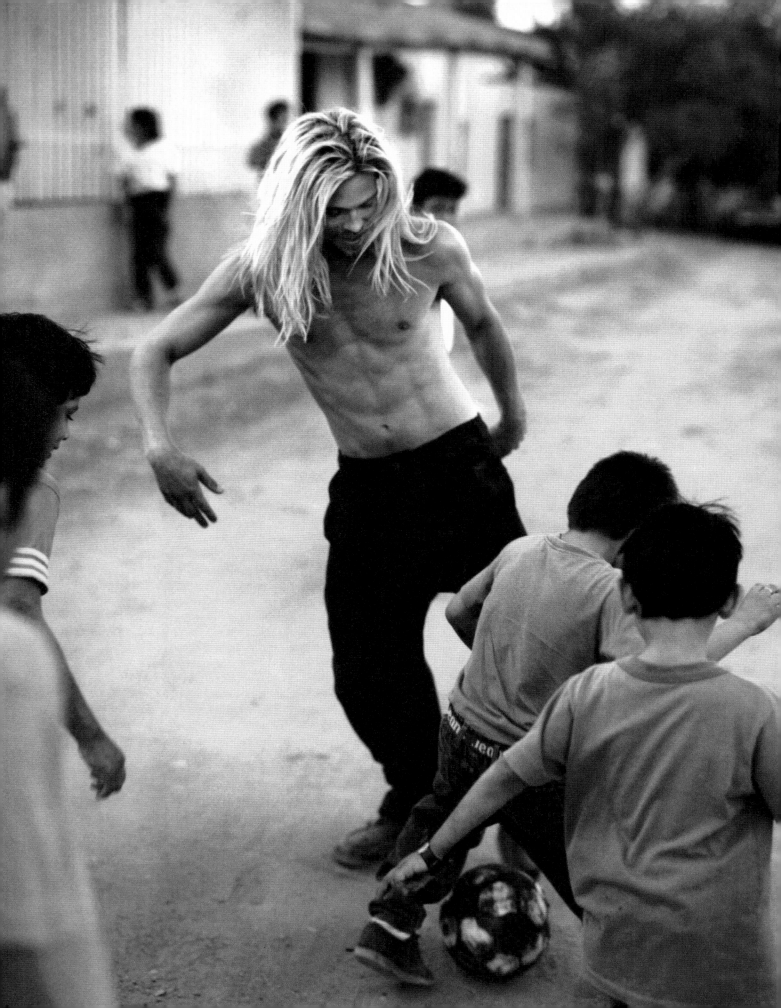

THERE'S SOME QUALITY THAT
BRAD HAS
THAT SHOWS SOMEBODY
WHO CAN BE QUITE
IRRESPONSIBLE,
BUT AT THE SAME TIME
HAVE A REAL SENSE
OF WANTING TO
NURTURE SOMETHING

Julia Ormond,
'LEGENDS OF THE FALL'
COSTAR,
January 1995

And so Pitt has purchased six hundred acres in the Ozarks where all his worlds can collide. The property will be a built-in destination during his periods of wanderlust, a spot near home where his family can convene with a little (at six hundred acres, more like a lot of) peace and quiet. And, to make things perfect, Pitt plans to design the home that will anchor his ranch.

Asked by a journalist where the property is, Pitt laughed. "Like I'm going to tell you? Yeah, right."

Here's another cliché:
I was in an acting class. A girl in the class needed a scene partner for an audition for an agent. So I was the scene partner for the audition, and I ended up getting signed.

– Brad Pitt, 1992

By the time he finally landed that agent, the future king of Hollywood was in need of a little luck. In Los Angeles for months, Pitt had been studying with an acting coach and covering the bills by shuttling strippers to appointments, delivering refrigerators to college students and handing out free cigarettes. He even got fired from a telemarketing job after only three days because he spent all his time chatting idly with the folks on the other end of the line and never made a sale. The only role he had landed was dressed as a chicken outside a fast-food chain called El Pollo Loco. Peering through a hole in the neck, Pitt emoted by flapping his wings to passing motorists.

"At the time it was all exciting," Pitt told *Rolling Stone* in 1992 with a straight face – maybe he was acting. But once he had an agent, Pitt soon snagged a recurring role on *Dallas,* and suddenly his fun in feathers was traded for a Screen Actors Guild card.

"I was living at an apartment in North Hollywood with eight guys, a two-bedroom apartment," Pitt told *US* in '95. "Two guys in the back room, two guys in the front room, four guys crashed out in the main room. No furniture. We all had our little corners, with our little books stacked, our little clothes folded, our little sheets. A little cockroach motel by the bed as a safety measure. We shared an answering machine. I got the part. I made a phone call to the folks. And basically just sat there and smiled."

Pitt's *Dallas* visit (he played "an idiot boyfriend who gets caught in the hay") lasted five episodes, more than enough time to turn some heads, among them costar Shalane McCall (whom he began dating) and the producers of *Another World,* the daytime soap opera where he scored a week of work. Offers to do Shakespeare, however, were not forthcoming. It was the Eighties, after all, and a look at Pitt's headshots from the time (porkpie hat, leather jacket, knowing pout) makes you thankful he wasn't recruited into New Kids on the Block. So he trudged on. Remember him in the *Growing Pains* episode entitled "Who's Zoomin' Who"? Well, no one does. But Pitt was there as a George Michael lookalike who tries to steal series regular Tracey Gold away from her boyfriend by taking her to see *Rebel Without a Cause.*

Next up was an episode of *Twenty-one Jump Street* (yes, he and Johnny Depp shared some onscreen cafeteria time) and a guest spot on *Head of the Class* that led to a romance (you'll begin to notice a pattern developing) with series star Robin Givens. Pitt was working steadily on television (he had roles on *thirtysomething* and *Tales From the Crypt*) as well as bagging the occasional B-movie role (*A Stoning in Fulham County, Happy Together, The Image* and *Cutting Class,* a teen slasher film Pitt happily refers to as "butt awful" in which he met future girlfriend Jill Schoelen). His career break may well have come from what *didn't* happen, however. Cast in a new Fox series called *Glory Days,* Pitt might have been trapped as Walker Lovejoy (seriously) had Fox not thankfully canceled the series, deciding there were only six *Glory Days* worth sharing.

"It was terrible," Pitt recalled in '94. "Man, I'd rather do nothin'."

Instead Pitt muddied himself up a bit for *Too Young to Die?*, an NBC movie of the week in which the former Walker Lovejoy played Billy Canton, a drug-addicted pimp who meets a fourteen-year-old girl and promptly hooks her on drugs and hooking.

"I felt I had to get something dirty to prove that I could do it," he told *Details* in '92. "I suddenly had a feeling that I knew I was going to get the part, weeks before, and I knew that whoever the girl was, that I was going to be very good friends with her. It's hard to explain, but I do trust my instincts."

Our psychic was right, and immediately after filming *Too Young to Die?*, Pitt and costar Juliette Lewis (who was sixteen to Pitt's twenty-five at the time) began a three-year relationship. Lewis recalled their meeting in a 1992 *Rolling Stone* interview where she was dubbed the magazine's Hot Actress:

"He was just really authentic," she said. "We drove back together [from Taft, California] – two hours of good, quality driving. We didn't say much. We listened to music. After that drive, we both knew we liked each other. We didn't even kiss. I was expecting it, because you move so fast these days. But he didn't; he gave me a hug. I tortured my best friend, Trish, over this for the next three weeks. Three weeks of, like, '*Oh my god!* What is he thinking?!' "

In the same issue of *Rolling Stone* (where, coincidentally, Pitt was named Hot Actor – not bad prognosticating) he talked about simultaneously wooing a girlfriend and shooting a film about drug addiction, prostitution and abusive relationships.

"It was quite romantic," he deadpanned. "Shooting her full of drugs and stuff."

As Lewis's career took off (she was an Oscar nominee for 1991's *Cape Fear)*, Pitt plugged away more slowly. He took a role as the straitlaced brother of the troubled Rick "Don't Call Me Ricky" Schroder in *Across the Tracks* – a performance that helped Pitt's credibility with casting directors if not the general ticket-buying masses. Pitt had been in Hollywood for five years, amassing a résumé and awaiting his first big break. It would come soon, but even in retrospect, Pitt respected the process.

"I hear people gripe all the time about coming to L.A. and not being taken seriously," he said in '94. "You've gotta show 'em. When I first started, I was being sent out on sitcoms. I like sitcoms, but I would be shitty in 'em. So I have to find something I can do and go out and get it. Then they go, 'Oh, he can do that.' But wait, there's more. I want to do *this* now."

He is extremely slippery – and don't let him fool you into thinking he doesn't know it. When Brad Pitt wants to throw you off, his voice will grow more down-home – an exaggerated version of his usual Ozarks drawl – and he'll toss out words like "dorky" or "wackadoo" to let you think you're simply swapping stories around the cafeteria table. Do not believe for a minute that Pitt doesn't realize what he's doing. Tom Cruise might have that grin, but Pitt has his Southern hospitality, and both are great protection, effectively drawing people in without ever allowing them to get too close.

This is not to suggest that Cruise's grin or Pitt's charm are contrived. Both, I am certain, are very real – integral parts of what helped make them stars. It is just that at critical moments grins and drawls make effective shields. And so when Pitt is open, he speaks of his movie roles or future goals in a quiet tone that comes from that part of Missouri that considers itself a Midwestern state. When he hopes to avoid speaking of his movie roles or future goals, however, Pitt sounds as if the great state of Missouri just up and joined the Confederacy. An interactive example:

You are Brad Pitt. You want to continue to be a nice person (because, it is critical to note, you are), but you feel like you have given too much of yourself for one lifetime. Someone (a journalist? fan? old friend?) approaches and suggests getting a cup of coffee. For the sake of the example, we'll choose the old friend.

Friend: "Do you want to grab a cup of coffee? I'd like to find out what's happening in your life!"

[At this point, you act as if this is a suggestion you never

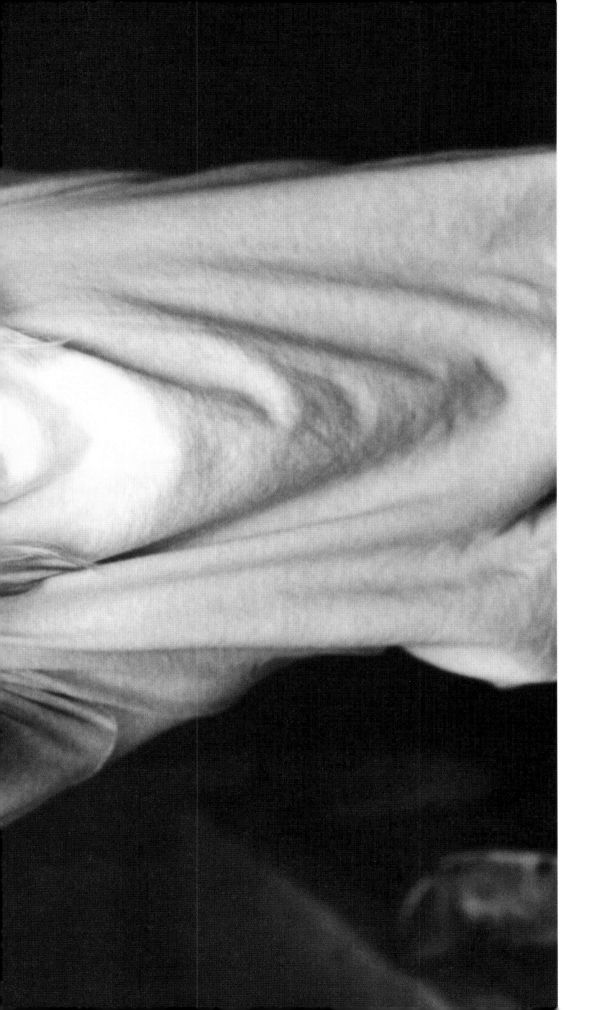

HEARTTHROBS ARE A DIME A DOZEN AND IT'S A KIND OF CLICHE. I DON'T THINK MUCH ABOUT IT AND IT DOESN'T MEAN MUCH TO ME THAT SOMEBODY CHOOSES ME AS AN OBJECT OF FANTASY.

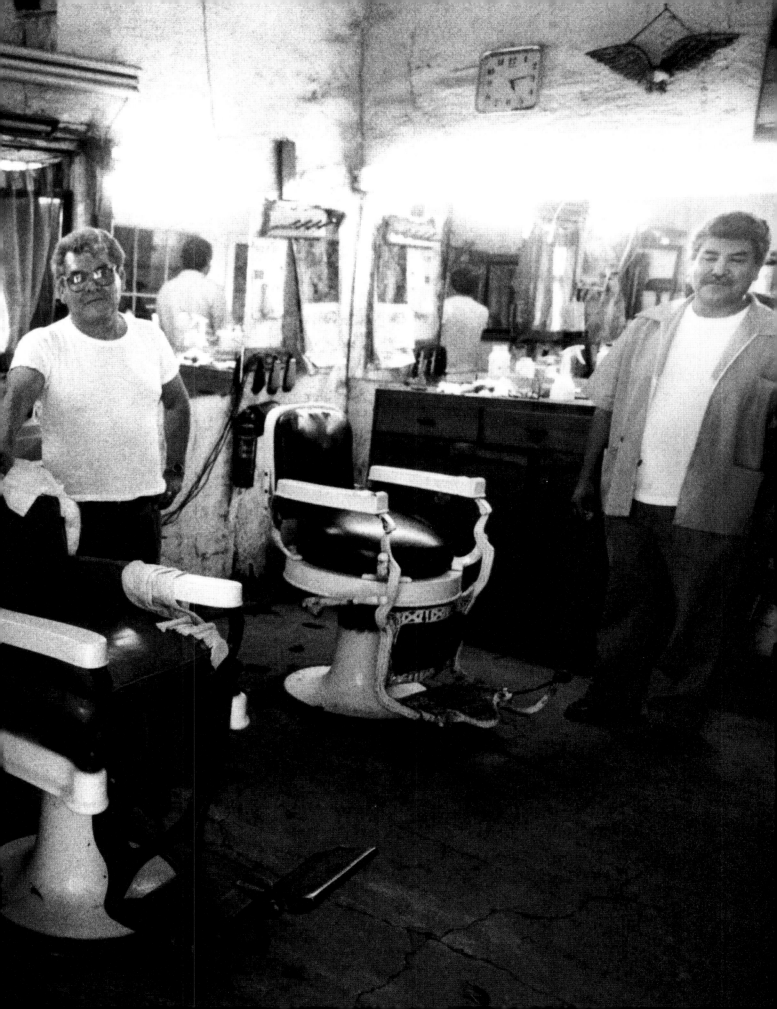

would have possibly considered. When you speak, you sound exactly like Pitt as J.D., the hitchhiker who charmed the pants off Geena Davis in *Thelma & Louise.* For the perfect pitch, please conjure up when he would turn away from the more cynical Susan Sarandon and say to Davis, "Now, *Miss Thelma."* Or better yet: "Well, now, I may be an outlaw, darlin', but you're the one stealin' my heart."]

You: "Outstanding. A cup of coffee?" You shake your head in amazement at the very notion of going out for coffee. *"Outstanding."*

Congratulations. You have just simulated a successful Brad Pitt evasion. After this, the conversation can skim the surface of any topic without your companion being any the wiser.

It is a painfully simple process, this illusion of intimacy, but the key to its success is that it must seem new each time. In conversation, as on film, Brad Pitt is charming, and he charms indiscriminately – young, old, male, female – until ultimately you are left wondering what is real and what is not. And this is simultaneously his best and worst quality.

Talk to anyone in the public eye and they will echo the sentiment that what is most difficult about the attention is knowing what to give and what to keep for yourself. Faced with a level of scrutiny shared by only a handful of people in the world, Pitt seems to have decided to play the role of the well-mannered, good ol' boy made good.

For the most part, it is a role for which he was typecast . . .

"People at Missouri were really surprised when they found out what Brad was doing," said his college friend Chris Schudy in 1994. "But he's always been so charming that it made some sense. The first time my mom met him, she called him a little Roman god."

. . . All Pitt has to do these days is turn the level up an extra notch and everyone is happy. No one gets hurt, the public is charmed, and he is safely distanced. A great deal of Pitt's captivating quality, in fact, comes from the fact that you *know* he's selling you a case of snake oil, but you simply don't care. You like him anyway.

For those of you afraid that this theory might not sit well with Mr. Pitt, don't worry. He might chew his bottom lip or kick his boots at the ground to disagree, but pay no mind. All the dust he kicks up is just a smoke screen. He knows what he's doing.

"I have to use a cheesy word, but I'd say I try to guide my

life by honesty," Pitt told me in 1994. "And that's a hard thing. I haven't mastered it by any means. I can be a lying shit sometimes."

I figured it would be a role like J.D. – something I'm good at, a Southern guy – that would make the break. It basically opened the door for some kind of respect, working with all those great people.

– Brad Pitt, 1992

It took Brad Pitt only five years of steady work to nab fourteen minutes of well-executed screen time and establish a career. Not bad for a kid who got sent out of his first acting audition with the words "Have you thought about acting lessons?"

The year was 1991, and the moment Pitt sauntered into the lives of Thelma and Louise, looking and acting almost exactly like the precocious Missouri kid that he was, everyone in Hollywood knew he had a future. Perhaps he was lucky. As the drifter J.D. who charms Geena Davis into bed, Pitt got much more attention for providing Thelma's first orgasm than for stealing her last dime. Or 60,000 dimes as it turned out. Dubbed the "$6,000 orgasm," the question of whether women would be happy to fork over all that loot for a sexual awakening was a staple in newspaper opinion polls and radio call-in shows. It certainly didn't hurt Pitt that when the question was asked, the women of America saw him as the man for the job. Then again, there was something more.

"Brad has kind of come into acting by being himself, hasn't he?" director Neil Jordan (*Interview With the Vampire*) told me in 1994. "He's come into it by being this incredibly charismatic character. But I think he's far better than he pretends he thinks he is. I think he's great, and I think he actually knows he's great. People are either stars or they're not. They either project it or they don't. The minute Brad walked into *Thelma & Louise* he did that. He was a star from then on."

The irony of Pitt's big break was that the role originally had been given to Billy Baldwin, but when the man most likely to marry Chynna Phillips backed out for a bigger role in *Backdraft,* the role fell to Pitt. To keep a semblance of consistency to his career thus far, the virtually unknown Pitt began a romance with his costar and major Hollywood player Geena Davis.

How that fits into the time line of Pitt's three-year relationship with Juliette Lewis is hazy, but after a short while the team of Pitt and Davis parted ways, and Pitt and Lewis set up house together in the Hollywood Hills. Both of their careers were now taking off; the *National Enquirer* was digging through their trash; they were frequently pictured as the apotheosis of the newer, grungier "I don't bathe, therefore I am" side of Hollywood; they were happy.

"We were trying to be Sid and Nancy or something," Pitt told me in 1994. "We were idiots. We were just having a great time."

As Pitt settled into his new quasi-domestic existence, he went back to work in *Johnny Suede,* a sweet, charming film in which he portrayed a pathetic rockabilly wannabe with an obsessive interest in suede shoes and Ricky Nelson, not necessarily in that order. When he spoke about the character to the *San Francisco Chronicle* in 1992, there were obvious connections to his own life and the parallel pitfalls he hoped to avoid.

"Johnny is a dilettante," said Pitt. "He feels that he has to put on this image and comb his hair that way in order to become someone. It's not so much that he's self-centered but

that he wants so badly to get things right – and he ends up walking around doing all that. . . . In the end he wakes up a bit and realizes he's been an idiot. But he's always trying – and that's what I like about him."

But beyond vague real-life similarities, *Johnny Suede* will always be remembered for two things. There is, of course, that hair: "I must say that I felt like an idiot walking around like a dork," said Pitt in the same article. "It took almost two hours every morning to get the look right." But most of all, *Johnny Suede* will be remembered because it is the film before *Living in Oblivion,* director Tom DiCillo's second feature about the horrors of making an independent film. *Living in Oblivion* featured a bumbling leading man who hits on all the women on the set and insists on excruciating take after take in order to hone his craft. The character's name is Chad, and many people – let's be serious, *most* people – insist that if the rhyme fits . . .

"We offered Brad the part," DiCillo told *Cosmopolitan* when *Living in Oblivion* was released, "so how could it possibly be spoofing him? He wanted to do it but couldn't because of scheduling problems. But he called me the other day, and we laughed about it. For some reason, everybody wants to believe that Chad is Brad, no matter what I say."

Anyway. Back in Brad Pitt's career, there was a brief moment of turbulence. It was called *Cool World,* a film in which he played a detective patrolling a cartoon universe to ensure that the Toons didn't have sex with humans. Most of his scenes were filmed against a blue screen, with his costars drawn in later, and if you think it all sounds a bit silly, consider that Kim Basinger spends the entire first half of the movie animated. Pitt attempted to explain the film to *Rolling Stone* in 1992. It went a little something like this:

"If you have an ego," said Pitt, "you'll lose it just having to do this." At this point Pitt put his hands around an invisible girl and kissed the air. "That'll humble you real quick."

During one of our interview sessions in Glasgow, I asked Pitt about his less-than-successful attempt at Saturday-morning cartoons.

"Ah, I really liked [director] Ralph Bakshi," he said. "I wouldn't want to say anything bad."

I told him that I realized everyone on a film, no matter what the results, feels territorial about the experience, but he could at least admit that it wasn't a rousing success.

New Orleans

"We all tried so hard on that movie," he said.

But that doesn't mean it worked.

Pitt leaned back and grinned. "Well," he said, "you haven't seen me in any more cartoon movies, now have you?"

{ A QUESTION OF CHARACTER ACTING }

Brad Pitt considers himself a character actor, not a star, and it is probably the fact that he cares about such distinctions that makes us care about *him*. Remember his thoughts about Johnny Suede: "He's always trying — and that's what I like about him."

Perhaps the best example of Pitt's commitment to altering his personas is the fact that he turned down an offer to play one of the astronauts in *Apollo 13* so he could star in the movie *Seven* — bypassing working with a two-time Academy Award winner (Tom Hanks) and star director (Ron Howard) in order to take his cues from a director (David Fincher) best known for music videos who wanted the actor to slog through a world of brutal ritualistic killings and ultimately find his wife's head in a box.

The fact that *Apollo 13* was an exceptional, well-directed, well-acted movie (when Pitt's mom saw it she called him and said, "You've gotta do more of these movies") misses the point entirely. *Seven* was also an interesting, well-directed, well-acted movie and, most of all, it was a gutsy choice, one that lets us know that Pitt is always trying — and that's what we like about him.

The *Apollo 13–Seven* distinction is by no means an isolated incident, nor is it a pretension that Pitt gained once he was able to choose whatever role he damn well pleases. Keep in mind that Pitt followed up his stint in sitcoms with *Too Young to Die?*, filmed *Johnny Suede* after *Thelma & Louise* and used the serial killer Early Grayce in *Kalifornia* to choke the life out of golden boy Paul Maclean from *A River Runs Through It*. It is no surprise then that *Seven* was filmed after his turn as a long-maned, horseback-riding hero in *Legends of the Fall*.

"He says he's a character actor, and I know exactly what he means," director Alan J. Pakula told *Detour* magazine in 1997. "Unlike many comparable big stars, especially of his generation, he takes chances. He does not just play a star persona. He tries to develop characters that are not obviously related to him, and in that way he's just a very serious, committed actor. At the same time, there is something about Brad that is deeply sympathetic, aside from the fact that he's obviously so attractive."

Oh, yeah, *that.* There is no doubt that much of Pitt's appeal comes after the word *sex* and a hyphen, but Pitt's onscreen characters are seldom as appealing as the man himself, and that is an important distinction. In 1992 — after he had finished filming *A River Runs Through It* but before its release — Pitt gave two interviews, to *Rolling Stone* and *Details,* that hinted that the road of his growing celebrity would be fraught with hairpin turns.

"The typical hero with the cool one-liners just doesn't interest me," Pitt told *Rolling Stone.* "I'd rather see people dealing with problems, trying to get around them. There's places for both kinds of roles, but what I respect is this thing of seeing people trying."

In *Details* Pitt continued the thought he'd started in *Rolling Stone,* albeit with his cards typically close to his chest.

'Details': "{*Agents*} *must be thinking that you'll never be this hot again and that you should be cashing in."*

Pitt: "*You can't just 'cash in.' It seems to me that you take a role . . . you take a role because there's something you kinda want to check out. You know? In your own mind."*

"*Can you give me an example?"*

"*No, I'm going to leave it at that."*

"*One example?"*

"*No, I think I dove too deep right there."*

And finally, in the *Rolling Stone* article, Pitt chronicled his Hollywood coming of age: "A funny thing happens that I just now became aware of, and I really believe it's why some actors don't keep doing what they started out doing. All of a sudden, these people are telling you that you're worth this, you're worth that. You're worth more than you feel, and what they're really telling you is that now you have something to lose. And so actors start operating out of fear; they're scared to do that, they're scared to do this, emphasizing all these other elements that have nothing to do with the art. It's a business, but business can't be the main emphasis."

If any of this sounds disingenuous, consider this: The only person who wants to be an astronaut more than a seven-year-old boy does, is a movie star.

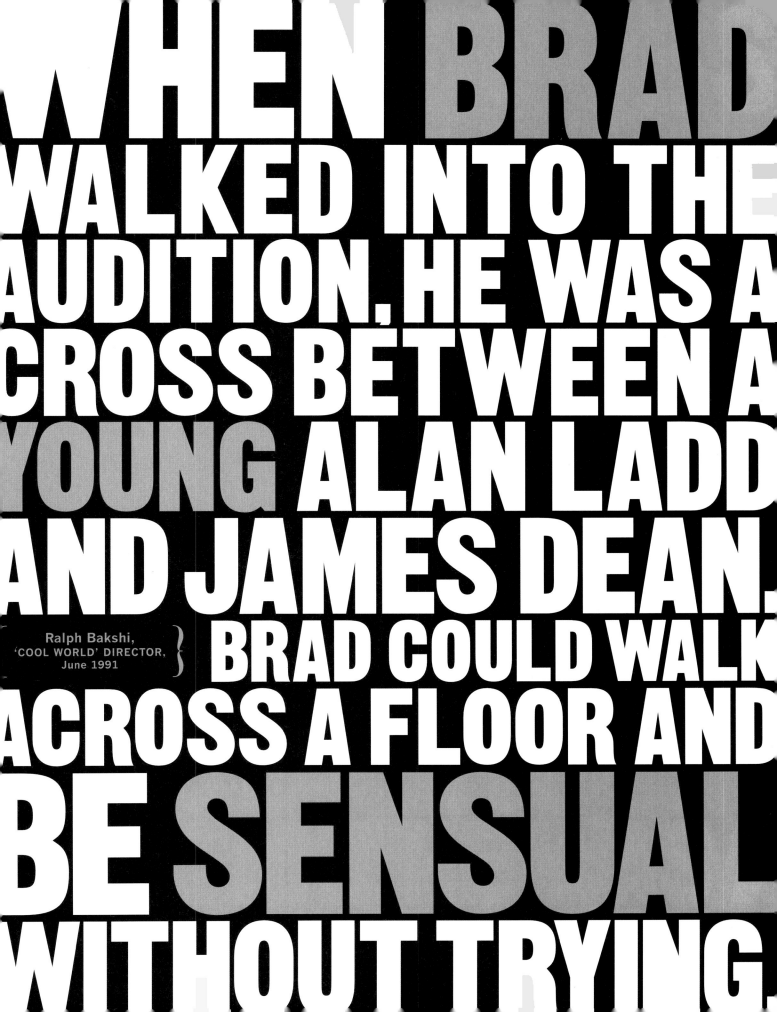

WHEN BRAD WALKED INTO THE AUDITION, HE WAS A CROSS BETWEEN A YOUNG ALAN LADD AND JAMES DEAN. BRAD COULD WALK ACROSS A FLOOR AND BE SENSUAL WITHOUT TRYING.

Ralph Bakshi,
'COOL WORLD' DIRECTOR,
June 1991
}

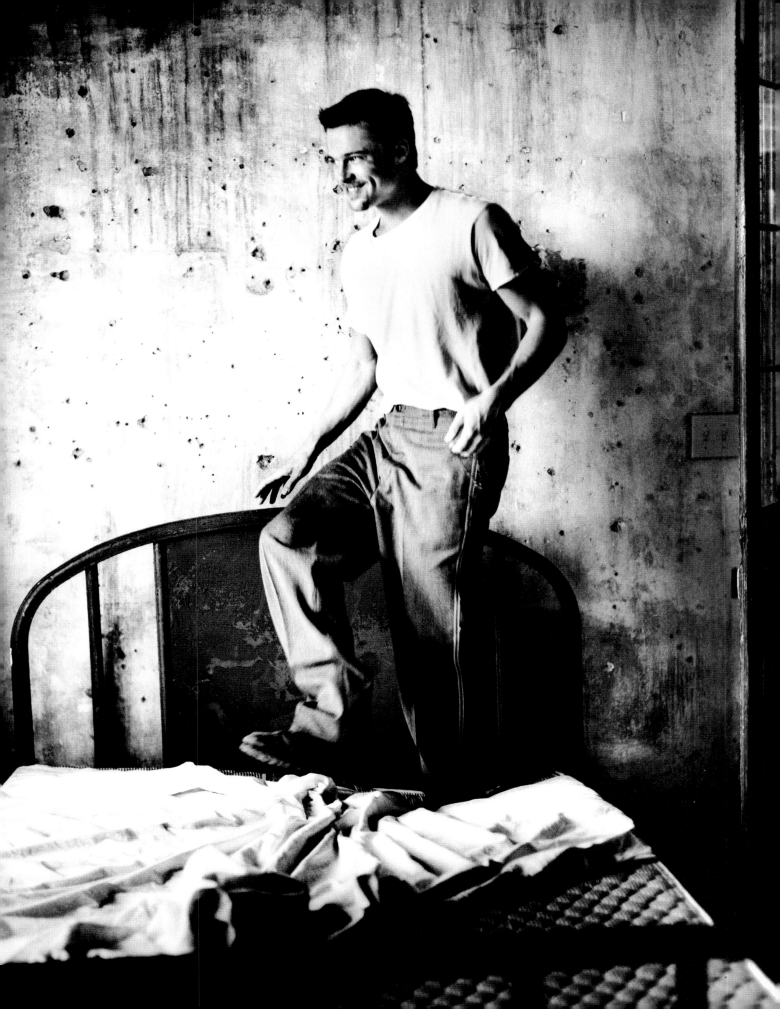

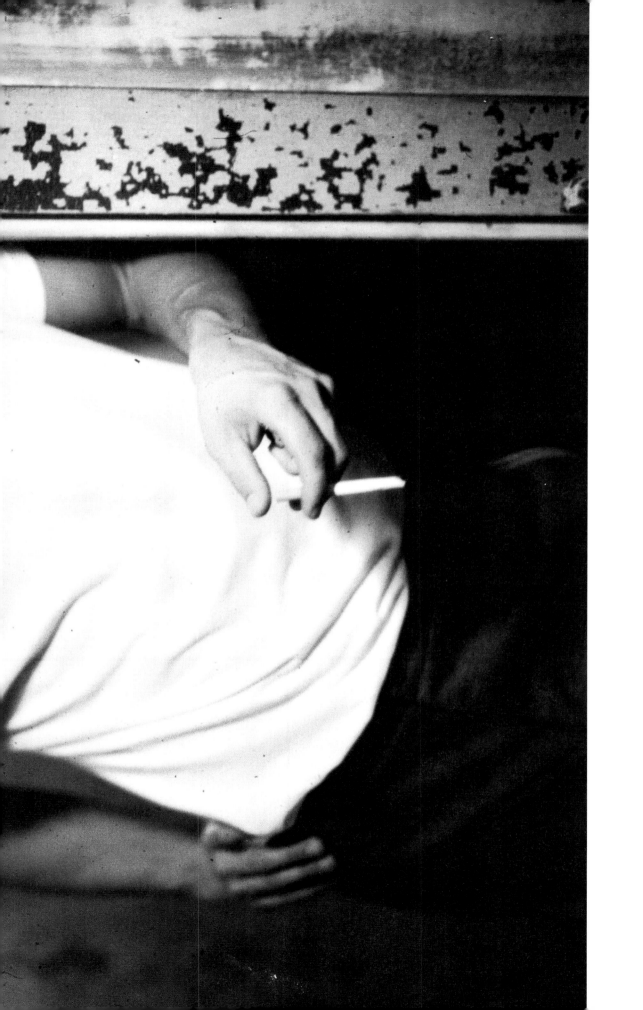

BRAD IS ONE OF THOSE RARE ACTORS WHO CARRY THEIR OWN LIGHTS. BY THAT, I MEAN BRAD IS COMFORTABLE IN HIS OWN SKIN

{ Edward Zwick, 'LEGENDS OF THE FALL' DIRECTOR, November 1995 }

It's like – do you play tennis at all? You know when you play with some-one better than you, your game gets better? I just kind of feel that way about it.

— Brad Pitt, on being directed by Robert Redford, 1992

Brad Pitt was not happy with the audition. He was nervous, slightly tense and felt that he could do better. And so Robert Redford told him that he could redo his two scenes for *A River Runs Through It* at home, on tape, and then send them in for a second look.

What Redford saw when the tapes arrived was Pitt and actor Dermot Mulroney in a short film featuring background music by Pitt's friend Melissa Etheridge and decked out in period costumes made by actress Catherine Keener, Mulroney's wife and Pitt's *Johnny Suede* costar. None of it really made an impression.

"It was not on the tapes," Redford told *Entertainment Weekly* in '92, of what led him to cast Pitt in the role. "It was in the office. Brad had an inner conflict that was very interesting to me. He's an extremely smart guy inside, quite sensitive, but it's all covered over with the part that needs to act tough to get along in the world. The way it comes out in his acting is very free, very raw. It's the way I like to work as an actor. So it was worth it to me to try."

And so Pitt landed the role of the fly-fisherman Paul Maclean and headed to Montana, where he and his costar Craig Sheffer drove through the state together. The road trip helped the pair bond as onscreen brothers and get acquainted with the local way of life that lay at the very heart of the movie they were about to make. When filming started, Pitt (who had rented a house) even set up a camp next to the river where he would make a fire and sit with his dog, eating food that he brought from the set. But for all his preparation – and the fact that the movie struck many familiar chords from his childhood – Pitt remains self-critical.

"I felt a bit of pressure on *A River Runs Through It*," he told me in 1994. "And I thought that it was one of my weakest performances. It's so weird that it ended up being the one that I got the most attention for."

Pitt's director hints that the young actor's analysis, while too hard on himself, is not terribly wide of the mark. "You were asking a guy who hadn't had much experience of being overt to make a big leap," Redford told *Entertainment Weekly*. "I'm quite proud of Brad's performance and I'm proud of myself for getting it from him. There were a lot of hurdles to get over.

"Brad was very rural, very laid-back. Very James Dean. That I didn't want. I wanted him healthy. Sunny. As vibrant as possible. In those days, when a good education was hard to come by, young people wanted to create the impression of being forward-thinking. They were likely to be much more demonstrative. And Paul was so comfortable with himself physically that I needed Brad to feel the same way – he had to do a lot of working out. He had to practice his fly-casting."

Once the film wrapped, Pitt headed home to Hollywood where, he first set up house with a pal he met while filming *A River Runs Through It* and then began living with Juliette Lewis. He also set to work on countering the beauty and

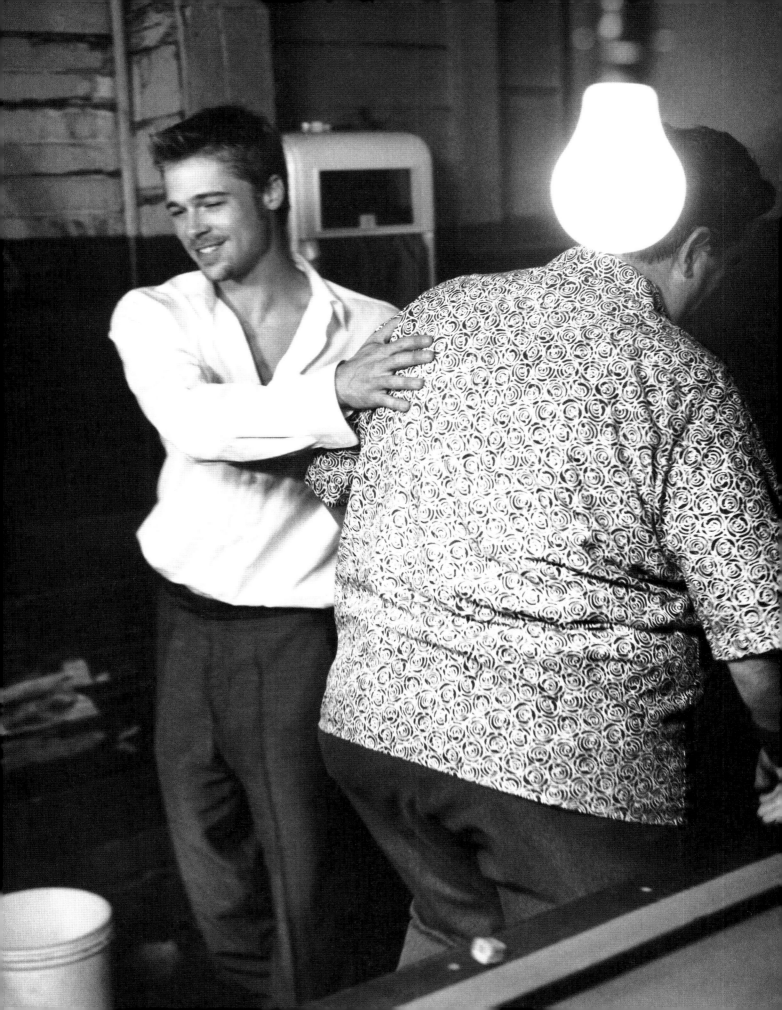

I THINK IT'S POSSIBLE TO BE BOTH A MOVIE STAR AND AN ACTOR—AND I'D LIKE TO BE THAT—BUT THE WHOLE MOVIE STAR THING **CONFUSES ME.** I DON'T THINK MY PERSONALITY SHOULD EVEN GET INTO IT. PEOPLE SHOULD JUDGE ME ONLY BY MY MOVIES

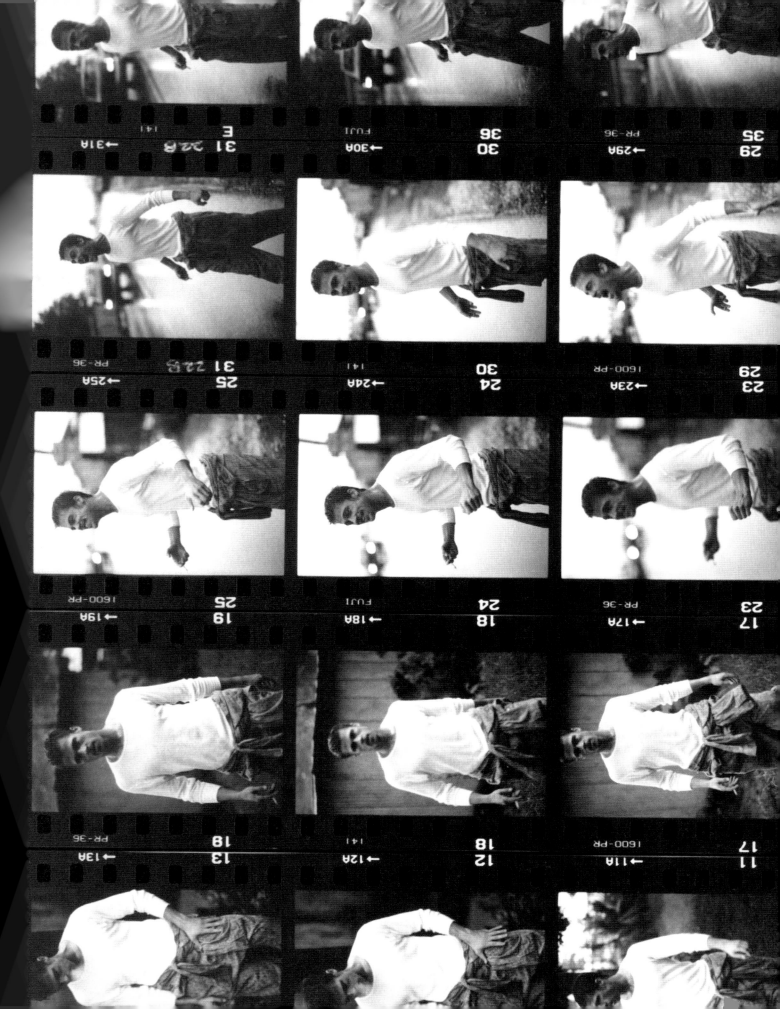

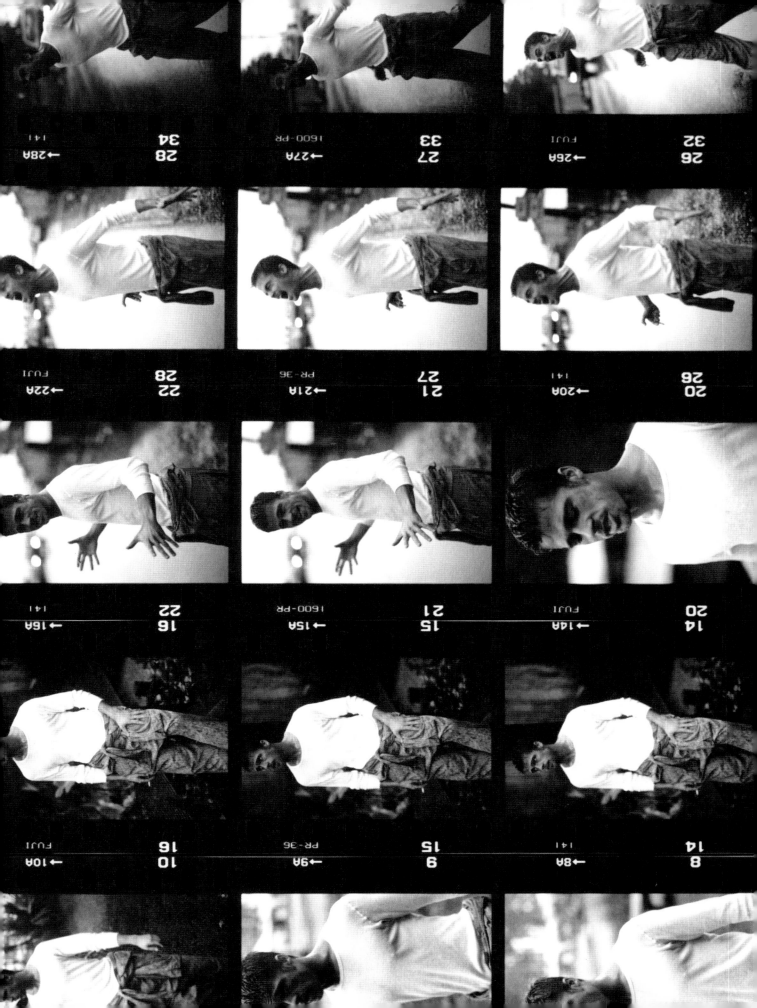

MY ANSWER TO EVERYTHING
THAT I DON'T HAVE AN ANSWER FOR IS
"DON'T TAKE EVERYTHING
SO SERIOUSLY."
THAT'S THE WAY I DO THESE
MOVIES
BECAUSE I HAVE OTHER THINGS
'D REALLY LIKE TO DO
THAT HAVE NOTHING

grace of alter ego Paul Maclean. ("As soon as you get an image," he told *Details,* "you gotta break it.") The answer was *Kalifornia,* the film about the cross-country jaunt of a serial killer that Pitt's agents begged him not to do.

Costarring Lewis and David Duchovny (later of *The X-Files), Kalifornia* is most notable as one of Pitt's many about-faces. He gained twenty pounds for the role; he chipped his tooth on a soda bottle to look more white trash; he wore a scraggly beard; he talked as if he had three tins of Skoal lodged between his cheeks and gums. In short, he made sure people wouldn't take to heart what was said onscreen of Pitt's character at the end of *A River Runs Through It*: "He was beautiful."

And lest we forget that Pitt is a character actor, he added an hysterical cameo as a twenty-four-hour stoner in *True Romance* that led college kids across America to start constructing bongs out of small plastic honey containers shaped like bears.

"That was fun," said Pitt at the time. "But I was only there for a couple days."

Around this time also came the release of *The Favor,* a movie Pitt had filmed three years earlier that, thankfully, has been forgotten. In fact, the most significant event of that period for Pitt was not captured onscreen. By the time *Kalifornia* was released, he and Lewis had broken up — marking the end of one life stage and the cusp of another. He was about to go to work on the two films that would change his life and career irrevocably and, suddenly, his partner of three years would not be along for the ride.

During the Scotland trip that made up a great deal of our 1994 interview, Pitt and I found ourselves in his hotel room getting ready to go out for the evening. The television was on, and we both looked up to notice Juliette Lewis onscreen kissing Johnny Depp in a scene from *What's Eating Gilbert Grape?* I stayed silent, not knowing what to say, as Pitt stared at the screen, smiling widely.

"She's really good in this," he said finally.

I asked him if it's difficult to see your ex-girlfriend on television when you least expect it, especially if she happens to be kissing Johnny Depp.

"Not at all," he said. "It's a nice way to see she's doing well."

He watched a short while longer, quietly, until it was finally time to leave. "She's such a good actress," he said again admiringly. And then he turned off the television and she was gone.

There has not been a more anticipated merger since ABC met Disney, a real-life fairy tale in a town that anyone who goes to the movies will tell you is desperate for quality fairy tales. It was evidence of this fanatic interest that, in December of 1996, Pitt graced the front pages of both newspapers and magazines when he announced he was engaged; just as it was a testament to the level of his stardom when, in June of '97, these same covers reported that, at least for the moment, the engagement had been called off.

And while this does not fit into the time line of events covered thus far — he has not yet filmed *Seven* and therefore hasn't even fallen in love with his fiancée — let's not get too caught up in chronology.

By this time you undoubtedly know the woman to whom Pitt was betrothed, but, for the sake of completeness, let us rehash. Her name is Gwyneth Paltrow and, at just twenty-five, she is already a formidable actor in her own right. Along with *Seven,* Paltrow has shone in roles as diverse as *Hook* (she was Wendy to Robin Williams's Peter Pan) and *Flesh and Bone,* the dark drama in which she played the girlfriend of older murderer James Caan. It was her starring role in *Emma,* however, that best showcased the odd mixture of loopy charm and privileged sophistication that she gained growing up as the New York private-school daughter of artistic parents.

"I was both in the realm of the acceptable world and also like a carny kid or a gypsy," Paltrow told *US* magazine in 1996. "On one hand, I had this great East Coast private girls' school education [she attended the Spence School, a prestigious all-girls prep school on Manhattan's Upper East Side]; on the other hand, I would go to rehearsals with my mother and sit barefoot and cross-legged watching her work."

The mother of whom Paltrow speaks is Blythe Danner, the Tony Award—winning actress who, along with husband Bruce Paltrow (the television producer responsible for, among other things, *St. Elsewhere,* one of the Eighties' best dramas) instilled in their daughter a built-in integrity mechanism.

"I saw my parents do quality work, and I think that just forces you to push for a higher standard," said Paltrow in *US.* "My mother probably could have been a bigger movie star than any woman of her generation, but she chose to stay home and be with the family. And I just respect her so much for that. She's a brilliant woman."

These days, Paltrow has already finished filming the drama *Kilronan,* with Jessica Lange, as well as an updated version of Charles Dickens's *Great Expectations* that costars Ethan Hawke and Robert De Niro. She had been in London working on *Sliding Doors,* a comedy-drama, when Pitt's publicist announced that the Paltrow-Pitt wedding (planned for late summer) was off.

Mostly there was shock from the many friends who insist Pitt and Paltrow were very much in love. The pair had a policy not to let two weeks go by without seeing each other, and as recently as the April *Rolling Stone* interview, Pitt was quoted as saying: "I can't wait for it. Walk down the aisle, wear the ring, kiss the bride. I think marriage is an amazing thing."

Sure, there were differences: She likes to go out, he likes to stay in; he watches the pay-per-view *Ultimate Fighting Championships* and she, well, doesn't. And, of course, there were pressures of public scrutiny. Those, however, had been weathered by the couple since the beginning of their relationship. "I can't allow the tabloids to alter any of this," Paltrow once told *US.* "I can't allow them to take the joy and freedom away."

It is a cruel irony that the relationship is now even more the domain of the tabloids. Which leaves us with nothing but questions, guesses and a difficult, private time that must be played out publicly. Friends say the couple is still talking regularly, and some are optimistic that the two could get back together. Everyone knows that in Hollywood the ending can always be rewritten at a moment's notice.

You gotta understand, my character wants to kill himself for the whole movie. I've never thought about killing myself. It was a sick thing. I don't like when a movie

messes
with your day.

— Brad Pitt, on 'Interview With the Vampire,' 1994

From the beginning, nothing about *Interview With the Vampire* was easy. For starters, Anne Rice, the book's author, took it upon herself to stage a one-woman publicity bonanza announcing that anyone in heaven or hell was better suited than Tom Cruise to play Lestat, the tale's central figure. And that was long before the movie even began filming.

By the time Rice finally stopped her wailing, *Interview* already featured the full spectrum of Hollywood horrors: five difficult months of filming, rumors of conflict between the film's stars and, finally, a real-life tragedy when River Phoenix, who was slated to play the interviewer, died of a drug overdose.

"I knew River a little, but I wanted to know him more," Pitt told me at the time. "His death affected everyone on the movie, but at the same time it was real personal. You gotta realize, River did a role in *My Own Private Idaho* that took it to a level that none of these other young guys have gotten to yet. I was really looking forward to him being on the set. It just seems like when we lost him, we all lost something special."

Although they were released in the opposite order, Pitt actually entered the fray of *Interview With the Vampire* immediately after filming *Legends of the Fall.* He was, as his director Neil Jordan described, "totally exhausted." When I first met him, near the tail end of the *Interview* shoot, he was at the breaking point. I asked how the film was going. "You know," he said, "*Legends of the Fall* was great." I asked him about working with Tom Cruise. "I'm tellin' ya," he said, "Antonio Banderas is the greatest guy." I asked for another drink. It was bound to be a long night.

"Movies have always been cowboys-and-Indians for me," Pitt finally explained months later. "But when they had offered the part to Daniel Day-Lewis, I heard his response was

that he didn't like what it would do to him. Look, he's one of my favorites, but I thought, *Jesus Christ, more actor bullshit.* Now I'd say I understand a little bit more of what he was talking about. When I read the book, I thought it was great, and I think the movie is great. I'm really proud of it. It's just that, for me, making the movie wasn't so great."

Much of that could be put down to the dark subject matter as well as the fact that, because vampires don't hang out with friends on the beach, most of the movie was shot during exhausting all-night sessions. What it didn't explain, however, were the rampant rumors of competition between Pitt and Cruise (who demanded a closed set), including one that Cruise insisted on wearing lifts in order to be the same height as his costar. In retrospect, the intensity of the gossip flow from a closed set was an excellent hint at Pitt's stardom to come. At the time, however, it led to a whole lot of explaining. Some examples:

"They're two very different actors," director Jordan told me of Cruise and Pitt. "And their characters were very different. Tom's character loves control and loves inflicting pain on Brad's character. Brad's character just wants to escape. In many ways, they related to each other the way their characters did."

After our interviews had been concluded, Pitt actually tracked me down in New York, so he could better explain his relationship with Cruise. "I tell you, the machine Tom runs is quite impressive," he said. "I wouldn't want to live like that, but still . . . Listen, if you want to stay on top, you've gotta stay on top. A lot of times Sean Penn's movies don't make any money. And in my opinion, Sean Penn is the best we have in that age group. So you can't sit and make Tom out to be the bad guy. Tom Cruise is good in this film."

He stopped.

"I like the guy, I honestly like the guy," Pitt said after a moment. "But at a point I started really resenting him. In retrospect, I realize that it was completely because of who our characters were. I realize it was my problem." He laughed. "People take everything so seriously. It's a movie and it's done."

Which, of course, set the stage for *Legends of the Fall* and that entrance. You know the one: Brad Pitt as Tristan Ludlow – the man with the soap-opera name and the supermodel hair – slowly trotting majestically into view on horseback as Julia Ormond melts into a puddle on the frontier plain. That entrance. *Interview With the Vampire* might have been a huge box-office success, but that moment helped ensure that Brad

Pitt was a presence to be reckoned with.

The irony of Pitt's star turn was that the movie's director (Edward Zwick) and producer (Marshall Hershkovitz) were the creators of *thirtysomething,* where Pitt had nabbed a one-line guest spot in his salad days of 1989. That moment was not lost on Hershkovitz. "He caused such a stir on the set," said Hershkovitz in *People* magazine after the release of *Legends.* "He was so good-looking and so charismatic and such a sweet guy, everybody knew he was going places."

And so, where everything about *Interview With the Vampire* was difficult, everything about *Legends of the Fall* was easy. Pitt has described it as "the only role I've ever had when I didn't think anyone else could do it any better," and the ease with which he dominated a movie full of great actors (Aidan Quinn and a surprisingly off-his-game Anthony Hopkins) suggests that Pitt was correct. The movie was made over a three-month period in Calgary, and Pitt even performed many of his own stunts – obviously more at ease on horseback than he later would be sleeping in a coffin.

When he returned to Los Angeles after almost nine straight months away, Pitt wasn't quite ready to sit back and wait to gauge the storm that was about to take over his life. The experience of back-to-back movies had left him wired with the notion that a moment was within the grasp of his Hollywood contemporaries, so Pitt (not yet even settled into his new home) set out to meet his peers.

"I met a bunch of people," Pitt told me, post–*Interview With the Vampire,* "and it was that whole competitive, look-over, high school cafeteria thing. It was a shame."

And so Pitt retreated quietly. He read scripts and waited for the aftereffects of *Interview* and *Legends.* By the time both films were released, Pitt was finally comfortably settled into his Hollywood Hills home. He was also a movie star.

{ FAME AND PUNISHMENT }

These days Brad Pitt owns a paper shredder. It was a gift from Bruce Willis, who said simply: "You're gonna need this, kid." You see, there is fame and then there is phenomenon. And it turns out Pitt is the latter.

"For a year and a half I hadn't noticed how weird it was," Gwyneth Paltrow told *US* magazine in 1996. "But now it's getting to be like the Beatles or something. When we were in

A FEW OF US
LESBIANS
WERE IN THE HOT TUB, WATCHING
THE GUYS PLAY
BASKETBALL IN THE POOL.
WE STARED AT BRAD AND
WE AGREED HE COULD CHANGE
} A WOMAN'S MIND. A
Melissa Etheridge,
January 1997
BEAUTIFUL MAN
INSIDE AND OUT.

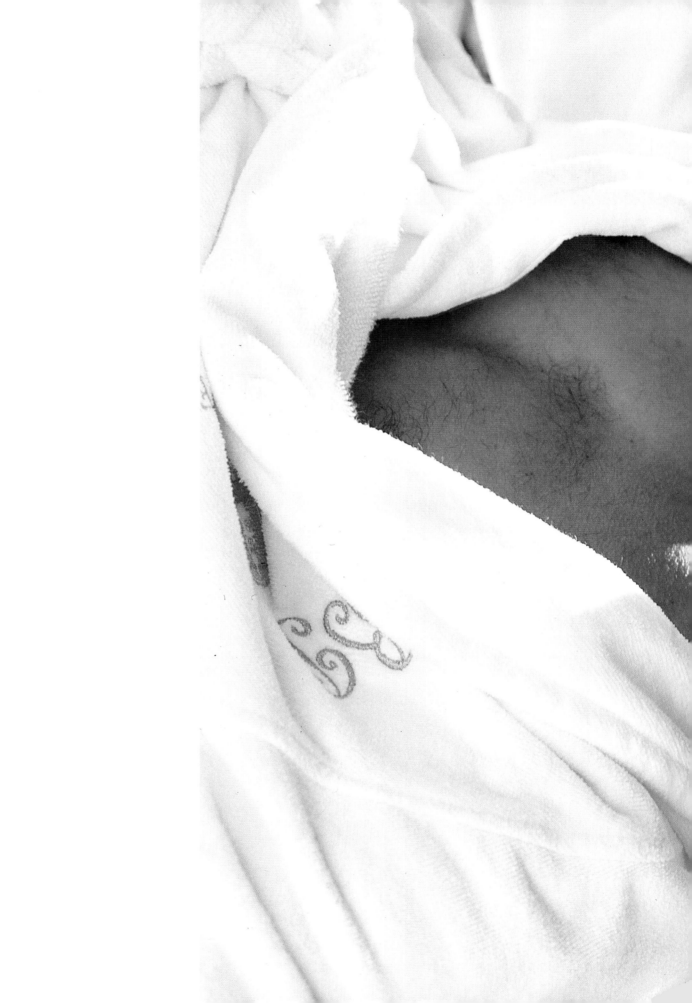

London last year [for the *Legends of the Fall* European premiere], these armies of little girls were standing behind gates, *crying.* Their faces were all contorted and beet red. It's getting crazier and crazier."

It can all be funny at times. Pitt couldn't help but laugh when he read rumors that he had donated his sperm to Melissa Etheridge and Julie Cypher in order for them to have a child. (They are close friends, but that's pushing things, don't you think?) He even began a battle of wills with a tour bus company that drove by his house every Sunday, only to have Pitt loft eggs at it.

"I thought that was fair," Pitt told *US* in 1995. "It's kind of a cat-and-mouse game."

But then a photographer took pictures of Pitt and Paltrow sunbathing naked on vacation in St. Bart's and sold the color photos across the globe; they eventually ended up on the Internet. Suddenly things weren't funny anymore. Pitt had tall trees planted around the perimeter of his yard, effectively ending his games with the tour bus; journalists were no longer invited into Pitt's home; and the laid-back kid from Missouri began looking into rights of privacy.

"The problem is that the laws have not kept up with technology," Pitt told *US.* "I understand where I'm sitting, and I expect every bit of it. But I wonder where the line is. . . . I've always taken everything pretty lightly, until we had these nude photos come out." He continued later: "Listen, ultimately it doesn't bother me. I mean, it all ends up in the litter box anyway. It *does* bother me that they take pictures of these private, special moments — something that's kinda sacred — and flash semi-naked pictures of my girlfriend. I find that that does not sit well with me. I see how it hurts her, you know? She wouldn't be going through this if she wasn't dating me." He shrugged. "But who really cares? I have one of the greatest jobs in the world, we see the country, our families are taken care of. I mean, there's a trade-off." He grinned. "If it means that I do a beaver shot so my kids will go to a good school, so be it."

The mania reached its peak on Pitt's most recent picture, *Seven Years in Tibet.* Filmed mostly in Argentina, Pitt was supposed to be portraying a man so at peace with himself that he ends up tutoring the young Dalai Lama. The only problem was that armies of Argentinians were making pilgrimages to get a glimpse of Pitt as if he were the Lama himself. Pitt might be at peace with himself, but that was all a bit much.

"On the first day, I invited him to a restaurant in a tiny village," said Jean-Jacques Annaud, the film's director, in a 1997 *Rolling Stone* interview. "There are two hundred fifty people living there. You have to get to the village by crossing two ropes." When the pair finally began eating, close to six hundred people began banging on the windows. Eventually, Pitt was forced to hire security and put a double barbed-wire fence around his rented home in order to keep people from scaling the walls. "It was starting to get ridiculous," said Annaud. "People would charter buses from Buenos Aires to come see the star. They were yelling and screaming, *'Braaaad!'* "

It made me recall something Pitt said in 1994, explaining that he didn't go out often. "I save wild nights for the road," he told me then. "Or I have wild nights at home."

With Pitt's fame inescapable on even the most remote roads these days, it appears that he is now left only with home. And, of course, his paper shredder.

Looove

'Seven.' I had such a good time on that film. That was probably the one I had the most fun on and the most sick one of them all, right? I had a gut feeling. Things were just falling into place; it just felt right.

— Brad Pitt, 1997

I DON'T KNOW [IF I'LL
ALWAYS BE AN ACTOR] I
DON'T KNOW IF I'LL ALWAYS
ENJOY IT.
I JUST WANT TO ENJOY
THINGS. I WANT TO ENJOY MY
DOG. I WANT TO ENJOY PEOPLE-EVEN
SILLY, STUPID PEOPLE.
I RESPECT
THAT SO MUCH MORE THAN
GETTING ANGRY ABOUT THINGS

’ll say. Let's review: Pitt's last two films dominated the box office, he moved into a dream estate and happily bided his time before filming *Seven,* which became a blockbuster against all odds and led Pitt to his future fiancée. Yes, things were falling into place and then some.

Still, it is difficult to consider the making of a film like *Seven* as a barrel of laughs. Unless of course you thought that *The Silence of the Lambs* got funnier every time you saw it. A serial-murder tale based on the seven deadly sins, *Seven* was notable as much for its brooding atmosphere and brutal depiction of murder scenes as it was for the interaction of the wiser, more distinguished Morgan Freeman and the wilder, more disheveled Brad Pitt. Murder victims were disfigured, fed until their stomachs burst and, ultimately, decapitated and delivered via courier. For all its success, *Seven* was not the feel-good movie of any season.

And then there was the fact that Pitt almost managed to become one of the dismembered. It happened during the shooting of a scene in which Pitt chases the murderer down a traffic-jammed street in the rain and runs across the hoods of cars. Everything was going fine and then suddenly: "I bit it," Pitt told *US* magazine at the time. *"Hard.* Basically, it was a matter of me trying to be cool and failing miserably. I slipped and went right through a car window. . . . My first thought, being the sick, twisted actor guy that I am, was like: *Oh, cool. I hope they got that."*

The accident shut down shooting for a short time and left Pitt in a cast for the rest of the film, forced to shoot many of his scenes from the side or with one hand tucked mysteriously in his pocket. Some actors keep souvenirs from their favorite roles. Brad Pitt got a long white scar across most of the knuckles on his left hand.

What Pitt also gained, however, was affirmation that his gut choices could be trusted to reap choice roles. He followed his turn in *Seven* with *12 Monkeys,* a dark foray deep into the psyche of director Terry Gilliam, the man who brought us, among other films, *Brazil* and *The Fisher King.* Pitt had to lobby Gilliam furiously to gain the role of a hyper-twitchy, hyper-paranoid mental patient.

"It was something that I normally wouldn't have been chosen for," Pitt told *US* in 1995. "And I understand that. People don't know what you're capable of until you prove it. So I met with him several times to try to get him to take a chance on me. And he did. And that was very cool of him, because he isn't into the name game. It's like, 'I don't care

who you are, cheesy movie guy.' He wants what's best. So he took a chance with me, and I appreciate that."

The gamble paid off. Whether it was the research time Pitt logged in a Philadelphia psych ward (only the ward director knew his identity, the patients were too involved in their own worlds) or the fact that Pitt had just been named *People* magazine's "Sexiest Man Alive" ("[Brad] found that appalling and was running as far away from that as possible," said Gilliam), Pitt nabbed a Golden Globe for Best Supporting Actor and an Oscar nomination for his work in *12 Monkeys.*

The accolades helped prove that Pitt was appreciated for attributes other than the ones that gave him star appeal. In fact, Pitt had greater success with *Seven* and *12 Monkeys* than with *Sleepers,* his next, more traditional role that was directed by Oscar winner Barry Levinson and costarred a pair of two-time award recipients: Robert De Niro and Dustin Hoffman. Not that Pitt's performance was bad. It's just that it's hard to shine in a film full of holes large enough to house a monster truck.

A revenge story wonderfully evoked in the film's childhood stages, Pitt's half of the movie, unfortunately, relies on Pitt's character (a prosecutor) being able to take a case without opposing counsel's noticing that he was a boyhood friend of the defendants. Pitt calls a needless witness (without rousing the judge's suspicions) who ends up harming his case. Then, Pitt's (and the defendants') other best friend just happens to sit in the front row of the courtroom clutching a copy of *The Count of Monte Cristo* so tightly that his knuckles turn white.

And if the screenplay dilemmas of *Sleepers* weren't enough, Pitt's next role – in *The Devil's Own,* opposite Harrison Ford – could have made a guy want to pack up his Nissan, drive back to the University of Missouri and finish up those last two credits.

In the end, it took six years and five different writers (the final writing credit had to be arbitrated by the Writers Guild) to come up with what Pitt resorted to telling *Newsweek* was "the most irresponsible bit of filmmaking – if you can even call it that – that I have ever seen. . . . We had no script. Well, we had a great script but it got tossed. . . . To have to make something up as you go along – Jesus, what pressure. It was ridiculous."

And then the real headaches began.

"I think Brad forgot for a minute that he was talking to someone who is paid to write this shit down," said Harrison Ford in *Entertainment Weekly.* Translated: He told the truth. Which is not always the modus operandi in a town kept alive by fiction.

Immediately, that interview (given to *Newsweek*'s Jeff Giles, who had also done Pitt's 1992 *Details* interview) became an outlet for all the frustration that the movie had helped build. Alan J. Pakula, the film's director, admitted in *Entertainment Weekly* that Pitt had tried to extricate himself from the picture. "He came in and panicked and said, 'This is not the film I want to make,'" said the director. "My feeling was, then let's see if we can get some gifted young Irish actor, get Harrison to stay and go ahead with the film." The only problem was that if Pitt pulled out, Columbia planned to sue him for $63 million. And so *The Devil's Own* kept going. And going.

"I would write dialogue in the trailer and an hour later hear the actors saying the lines," Robert Mark Kamen, one of the script doctors, told *Entertainment Weekly*.

Ironically, *The Devil's Own* eventually garnered decent reviews, albeit ones that often praised the fact that it was at least watchable, considering its many disasters. It also, however, opened with strong box-office numbers, leading to *Entertainment Weekly*'s final thesis: "Brad Pitt's bankability now seems unquestionable. He dissed his own film and *still* didn't kill its opening."

{ THE LAST WORD }

I break everything into stages," Brad Pitt told me in the summer of 1994. "There've been some good healthy stages and some that are really unhealthy. And I'd say, right now, I'm just getting out of the moron stage."

It is now three years since he uttered those words, and Brad Pitt, recovering moron, is progressing nicely. He still takes things one day at a time, of course, but he has eased into a more settled existence and is able to pick and choose any role his gut reaction desires. His next project will be *Meet Joe Black* (an update of the 1934 classic *Death Takes a Holiday*), which he was filming in New York during the time his engagement was broken. The status of his next scheduled film, *Duets* (an ensemble piece originally planned to costar Paltrow and be directed by her father, Bruce Paltrow), is unknown.

What *is* known is that before we see him in anything else, Pitt will be on our neighborhood big-screen in *Seven Years in Tibet,* the true tale of mountain climber and Olympic ski champion Heinrich Harrer. In 1939, Harrer and a partner (played in the movie by David Thewlis) attempted to climb one of the highest peaks in the Himalayas, only to be trapped in India and imprisoned by the British. After eventually escaping (by crossing the Himalayas) Harrer sought refuge in Tibet, where he became the tutor of the young Dalai Lama. It is a fascinating story of a multifaceted man, but if you ask the film's director, it's not just a movie, it's a metaphor.

"I was absolutely charmed by the reasons Brad liked the screenplay," Jean-Jacques Annaud told *Detour.* "I felt it was comforting that he not only understood what it was about, but it was also something that he wanted to sort out for his own life: fame and success versus respect and self-respect."

That is the stage at which Pitt finds himself today. So much has changed, yet in many ways his central questions haven't wavered. He still seems obsessed with building a career of significance without sacrificing his self-esteem. "If you ask me if money changes people," he told *Rolling Stone*'s Jancee Dunn in early 1997, "I'd say that money changes other people." And if this is correct, the key for Pitt these days is finding folks who still recognize him as a kid from Missouri and not a millionaire from the Hollywood Hills.

It is true that Pitt speaks more fondly of Los Angeles these days. "Aaah, it's nice there," he told *Detour.* "I like it 'cause so much has happened for me there. That's where I went and that's where I discovered a lot of things. I love it so much." But he is still guided as much by his wanderlust as he is by his need to be at a home base.

When we sat in his new home in 1994, boxes filling the downstairs corridor, Pitt gave the impression that he very much wanted his motives to be understood without having to reveal the underlying details of his life, and thus far he has been relatively successful. I asked if there was a responsibility that came with celebrity. "There is a responsibility there," he said. "I just haven't figured out what it is yet."

It's not likely that Pitt has any clearer idea today. He once said that "you take a role because there's something you kinda want to check out. You know? In your own mind." If Annaud is correct, Pitt's role in *Seven Years in Tibet* proves that answers don't always come so easily.

And so this book ends in the middle of what is sure to be a long and interesting career. The story is, in a great television tradition: *To be continued.* Undoubtedly there will be many more stages to come, but if Brad Pitt has any idea what they are, he is, as usual, not saying a word.

WHY I GO Gaga FOR Bra

gaga

{ By Lorraine Ali }

I'm not a girl
who falls for the selected pinup boy of the month. I never thought Tom Cruise was cute or saw Antonio Banderas as good-looking or considered Bruce Willis even remotely attractive. But Brad Pitt slipped under my savvy girl-of-the-Nineties radar, one that detects a packaged hard sell from a mile away and rejects it as

fast as a coin-operated machine does a slug. He penetrated my jaded exterior, tugged on that swoony, blubbering-fan chord in me and elicited the same brand of twinkly-eyed adoration that drove Lucy and Ethel to pull ludicrous stunts in front of Cary Grant and William Holden.

Though I don't think I'd attempt to sneak into Brad's house and hide under a bear rug or steal his footprints from the Chinese Theater (they're not there anyway), I will go and see any movie he's in. That's a big commitment for a gal like me who grew up around Hollywood and knows everyone is actually someone else. I'm convinced that most of Hollywood's outdoorsy, shirtless male leads who gallantly defy corrupt authority to fight the good fight are really Scientologists or, worse, Perrier-drinking vegetarians with personal trainers.

But Brad's different. I realized that the first time I saw the twenty-seven-year-old actor as the lean, convenience store–robbing cowboy in 1991's *Thelma & Louise.* He was sexy, trashy and dangerous, and looked really good in tight jeans –

the perfect sexual tidbit for an outlaw girl who doesn't have time for a relationship. He was only in the movie for a total of fourteen minutes but made enough of an impression to prod several post-movie references and make my boyfriend jealous. But it didn't end there.

I later saw Brad in the not-so-famous movie *Kalifornia,* yet had no idea he was the same actor who had made Thelma sizzle two years before. He played a delusional serial killer who takes a cross-country ride with his white-trash girlfriend (Juliette Lewis) and an art-schoolish couple (*The X-Files'* David Duchovny's big break). I liked the movie, but here's the sick part: The whole time Brad was making weird, phlegmy noises in his throat, leering at Duchovny's girlfriend and generally being a pig, I was thinking, *Hey, he's cute.* So what if he blew holes in a few undeserving folk?

I began seeing short interviews and photo spreads of Brad here and there. Sans the grubby criminal exterior, he was almost too conventionally good-looking and clean for my tastes. His chin looked a little too chiseled, his eyes a little too blue and his lips almost too puckered and ready to go. Also, the fact that he was becoming a heartthrob confirmed that I had been duped. I definitely should not like Brad. It worked for, like, a week, till Brad disarmed me. He's just so unpretentious, so comfortable in his own skin, so not like the rest. He exudes a well-balanced, Midwestern sensibility coupled with a slightly dangerous sexuality. It's a combo that even elicited an animalistic noise outta my mom: "I don't know what it is about him, but *grrr.*"

The only other actor who doesn't have to convince me to like him is Johnny Depp. Unlike Brad's, Johnny's allure — beyond his beauteous face — is his inner darkness. He is seemingly filled with miles of bruised, fucked-up sadness for a girl to dive into and become hopelessly entangled. But liking Johnny and Brad simultaneously is like choosing between evil and good, dark and light, decadent and fat-free. While Johnny fulfills a deep, dysfunctional need, there are times when you need the less-complicated, low-maintenance Brad. You get no sense of deep pain experience from Brad, no sense of disruptive behavior. That doesn't mean that he's a bad actor. He does transport me beyond his good looks and make me follow the plot, it's just I'm reminded at certain turns of his head and hips that I do have a ridiculous crush on this unreachable celebrity figure. How embarrassing.

My adoration did falter when Brad played concurring heartthrob roles in two big Hollywood stinkers, *Legends of the Fall* and *Interview With the Vampire*. The first was so long and boring that by the time Brad's manly, windswept character wrestled a grizzly, I was rooting for the bear. Someone had to kill off this one-dimensional character and free Brad from the role. The vampire movie was worse: In a film that could've been so creepy-cool, Brad was cast with jocko Tom Cruise (major points off), and the two struck more come-and-get-it poses than a *Baywatch* lifeguard. So what if there

were a few blue veins running through their foreheads — they still looked like underwear models. Both movies and characters sucked, and I think Brad knew it. I respected him for failing miserably at these cardboard cutout roles. It was enough to make me begrudgingly see one of his next films, *12 Monkeys*. Playing the psycho, drooling offspring of a mad scientist, Brad redeemed himself.

My pivotal moment of Brad Pitt fandom came during *Seven.* I hated the movie (it's hard to enjoy a film that enjoys rape, death and cruelty so much) but came to a huge realization about my adoration for the actor somewhere between the guy-tied-to-the-bed-for-a-year scene and the head-in-the-box scene. It was there Brad actually got to me on the last level of fandom before stalker behavior sets in — the boyfriend level. For all the times the actor crashed down doors, jumped fire escapes and partook in impossible gunfights, the most indelible moment was when he laid curled up in a sleepy ball with his real-life girlfriend and scripted wife Gwyneth Paltrow. It looked so plausible, so sweet, so loving and comfortable, and it exposed an ultra-human side of Brad I had formerly missed. It was like when Johnny Depp laid down with the dead baby deer in *Dead Man* — pure sweetness and devotion that superseded anything a camera or director could manipulate.

You have to be a cool guy to have had a sassy and smart girlfriend like Gwyneth. When critics recently bagged on him for his depiction of an IRA member on the run in *The Devil's Own,* I thought they were just jealous and wanted to be running hand in hand through daisy fields with Paltrow themselves. But I guess I'm no different on the Brad end of the devotion quotient. I hate the fact that I am merely one of a billion women who pine over Pitt. Not because I'm weird and obsessive and want the guy all to myself, but because it proves I am not the individual I think I am. I'm one more guppy chasing after the Babe 101 lure, willing to slap down eight bucks for his next film, regardless of its premise or promise. Which, by the way, should be released soon. ▫

THE IDEAL AMOUNT OF **TIME TO BE a SCREEN IDOL** IS SEVEN MINUTES. IT'S A **LITTLE BIT MORE THAN FIVE MINUTES BUT A LOT** LESS THAN TEN. **a FRIEND INSISTED I WAS VOTED SEXIEST** moron aLIVE.

~ *Brad Pitt, 1992*

THE MOVIE REVIEWS

THELMA & LOUISE

Rolling Stone, *April 18, 1991*

CALL IT A COMEDY of shocking gravity. *Thelma & Louise* begins like an episode of *I Love Lucy* and ends with the impact of *Easy Rider.* It's a bumpy path between those points, and director Ridley Scott *(Black Rain)* and first-time screenwriter Callie Khouri don't cushion the ride. The film switches moods violently, and sometimes it just jerks your chain. But this is movie dynamite, detonated by award-caliber performances from Geena Davis and Susan Sarandon in the title roles.

Davis plays Thelma, an Arkansas housewife married to a cheating, verbally abusive salesman named Darryl (broadly caricatured by Christopher McDonald) whom she began dating when she was fourteen. "He's an asshole," says Thelma, "but most times I just let it slide."

Sarandon plays Thelma's pal Louise, a waitress who is pushing forty and fed up with waiting for her musician boyfriend, Jimmy (subtly detailed by Michael Madsen), to stop roving and commit. Louise organizes a weekend fishing trip for herself and Thelma, who doesn't know how to fish. "Neither do I," says Louise, "but Darryl does it – how hard can it be?"

That's the setup: two women putting drudgery and men behind them for a few days of rest and intelligent talk. But before they reach their destination, a hungry Thelma asks Louise to stop her '66 T-Bird convertible at a roadhouse, where Thelma knocks back three shots of Wild Turkey and dances with a local Romeo.

Louise thinks her friend is just blowing off steam until she catches the guy beating and trying to rape Thelma in the parking lot. Grabbing Darryl's gun (which Thelma brought along for protection), Louise presses the barrel into the rapist's neck and says, "Just for the future, when a woman's crying like that, she's not having any fun." He hitches up his pants and starts to leave but not before saying to Louise, "Suck my cock." Louise takes two steps back and fires a bullet into his face. The suddenness of the act – the man is no longer a threat – is shattering. Vividly shot by Adrian Biddle

(Aliens) and edited by Thom Noble *(Witness),* the scene is made even more potent by Louise's whispered remark to the bloody victim: "You watch your mouth, buddy." In a stunningly poignant performance, Sarandon shows that the emotionally bruised Louise has been in a similar position before and has finally been pushed to her limit.

The dazed women drive off and try to plan their next move. The cops have staked out their homes. When Thelma phones Darryl, detective Hal Slocumbe (Harvey Keitel) urges the pair to stop running. Hal is the film's one sympathetic male character, and he doesn't ring true. Khouri – a Texas-born actress, video producer and former waitress – doesn't turn her movie into a man-hating tract, but she does show what a lifetime of male sexual threat and domination (disguised as paternalism) can do to women.

As Thelma and Louise – now outlaws – attempt to escape to a new life in Mexico, the movie offers vignettes that are comic, tragic and surreal, sometimes simultaneously. They pick up J.D., a hitchhiking hunk charmingly played by Brad Pitt. Thelma takes him to bed because she likes his body. "You could park a car in the shadow of Darryl's ass," she tells Louise. For once, Thelma has a sexual experience that isn't "completely disgusting." In bed, J.D. – using a hair dryer as a gun – teaches Thelma the art of armed robbery. Then he robs her. The experience pushes Thelma over the line; she knocks over a convenience store using the J.D. method. "I know it's crazy," she tells Louise, "but I just feel like I've got a knack for the shit." Swilling booze and howling like a dog, Thelma heeds the call of the wild. But Davis, who has never been better, keeps Thelma rooted in reality. Crime has taught her to express herself; she won't go back to a cage.

Surrender doesn't suit Louise, either. She knows the police won't buy the truth because "we just don't live in that kind of world." Besides, she says, "I don't want to end up on the damned *Geraldo* show." The banter doesn't disguise the terror these women feel, but driving through Utah's Canyonlands – after blowing up the gas tank of a semi whose driver offered to lick them all over – they achieve a kind of serenity.

As the film plunges toward its lacerating climax, some may have conflicting feelings about Thelma and Louise: Are they feminist martyrs or bitches from hell? Neither is the case. They're flesh-and-blood women out to expose the

blight of sexism. Khouri's script isn't about rage or revenge; it's about waste. Director Scott, whose films are noted for their slick surface, cuts to the marrow this time. This wincingly funny, pertinent and heartbreaking road movie means to get under your skin, and it does.   ~*Peter Travers*

US, *June 13, 1991*

THELMA & LOUISE' IS A KNOCKOUT. This briskly paced adventure comedy has everything a movie needs – intelligence, energy, humor, daring. And it moves in incredibly surprising directions – from belly laughs to sudden violence, from the comic to the epic to the apocalyptic. Unlike most movies, *Thelma & Louise* gets bigger and better as things go along. Without a doubt, it's director Ridley Scott's most vivid film since *Alien* – and it's a much richer piece of work.

On the most basic level, *Thelma & Louise* is a road movie. And like any road movie, it's about self-discovery. Susan Sarandon and Geena Davis play a pair of southwestern gal pals who take a three-day vacation from the men in their lives. They hit the highway acting guilty and giddy – as if they are cutting class. But things take a surprising turn when one of them is nearly raped in a roadhouse parking lot. The would-be rapist is killed, and suddenly the movie becomes a hair-raising run from the law, a feminist *Bonnie and Clyde*. Although Sarandon and Davis begin as careworn cohorts, they end up more like warriors – tall, tanned, exalted. You've seldom seen sister power like this before.

Susan Sarandon has had a gutsy career, and this may be her riskiest role ever. As a burnt-out waitress, she flaunts her age without sacrificing her sensuality. And she segues from sadness to delight with more dexterity than most movie stars can manage. Playing off Sarandon, Geena Davis scores her own personal best. Her character is the one who has the farthest emotional distance to travel – from dippy housewife to coolheaded thief. Using her puttylike features to great advantage, she undergoes a transformation that is exhilarating and utterly convincing. From a solid supporting cast, Brad Pitt makes the strongest impression. Pitt does a lithe, steamy turn as the hitchhiking hunk who teaches Davis the truth

about sex. He's the only one who can compete with Sarandon and Davis for sheer erotic charge.

Miraculously, this movie knows how to handle its darkest themes without ever losing its sense of humor and reckless adventure. Ridley Scott has always been an able stylist, a master of mood and surface, but this time he digs down deep. He works hard to give this story scope and substance. He jampacks his frames with revealing bits of business, little background stories that echo the main plot. Of course, from the director of *Blade Runner* and *Black Rain,* we expect stunning visuals, and as Thelma and Louise rush toward the Mexican border, Scott gets every drop of majesty and magnificence from the sun-drenched southwestern landscape.

Much of the credit for this movie should go to first-time screenwriter Callie Khouri. Her script is an unbridled piece of work. Khouri doesn't feel the need to force her characters into a corner before she permits them to lash out. Her plot assumes a backlog of female anger that the audience will understand, accept or – at least – allow. Khouri is not very generous to the men onscreen, and for that, the film may split the audience down the middle. Some will say that the movie goes too far. And to tell you the truth, it does. Still, you've got to love a big-budget picture that follows such a risky agenda and carries it right through to the final freeze frame. During a time when filmmakers are increasingly afraid to challenge the audience by taking a stand, *Thelma & Louise* has courage to spare. It is clearly the bravest, most breathtaking American film since *GoodFellas.*   ~*Lawrence Frascella*

JOHNNY SUEDE

Rolling Stone, *September 3, 1992*

THE BUILDUP – Best Film at Locarno, a smash at Sundance – may overstate the charms of this playfully hip comic fable starring Brad Pitt as a musician with a Ricky Nelson fixation. But there's no denying the kick of Pitt's memorably offbeat performance and writer-director Tom DiCillo's stylish debut. DiCillo had worked as a cinematographer, most notably on Jim Jarmusch's *Stranger Than Paradise,* and the Jarmusch influence can be seen in the film's spare, desolate setting, meant to reflect the fringes of an untamed American city (the film was shot in New York). Johnny, in a pompadour and suede shoes, roams this decaying metropolis looking for a dream job (playing music instead of painting apartments) and a dream girl. He thinks he's found her in Darlette (Alison Moir), whose mother (the spirited Tina Louise) is a record producer. But Darlette and Mom soon tire of Johnny's retro routine.

In this cynical world, the immature Johnny is innocent, despite flaws ranging from vanity to nervous flatulence. Pitt is a sensation, bringing deadpan humor and touching gravity to a role that could have been a cartoon. If Johnny grows up at all, it's due to the hard lessons he learns from an insolent pop idol, Freak Storm (a hilariously wicked Nick Cave), and a no-bull teacher, Yvonne (the fine Catherine Keener), who loves him. Though the film is no more than a series of striking vignettes, DiCillo strings them together with a vibrant inventiveness that makes you eager to see what he's up to next. ~*Peter Travers*

a river runs THrOUGH IT

Rolling Stone, *October 29, 1992*

TO READ NORMAN MACLEAN'S 1976 novella about families and the relation of fly-fishing to religion and art is to be held in thrall. Robert Redford certainly was. Now he's directed the film version from a script by Richard Friedenberg, who also wrote, yikes, *Dying Young*. Though Redford doesn't act in the film, he delivers the narration – much lifted from the book – with uncommon feeling. His reverence is both a blessing and a curse. Maclean, who died in 1990, was a retired English professor when he wrote this memoir, and cinematographer Philippe Rousselot invests the film with shimmering beauty of time remembered. Norman (Craig Sheffer) and his brother Paul (Brad Pitt) live in a Montana home tended by their mother (Brenda Blethyn) but dominated by their father (Tom Skerritt), a Presbyterian minister. Only when fishing the Big Blackfoot River using Dad's metronome casting rhythm are the men united. Faced with tragedy, the father still can't speak his heart. The director of *Ordinary People* knows this territory, and he draws delicately shaded performances. But in relying on narration, Redford's movie is too little show and too much tell. ~*Peter Travers*

US, *November 1992*

AS A DIRECTOR, Robert Redford is clearly drawn to a world of Protestant restraint. But where his 1980 Oscar winner, *Ordinary People,* was a gentile indictment, *A River Runs Through It* is a vague, New Age ode. Based on a cherished novella by Norman Maclean, the film takes place in Montana, circa 1930; it concerns the fly-fishing sons (Craig Sheffer, Brad Pitt) of a Presbyterian minister (Tom Skerritt). The movie is graceful and devotional, but it seldom echoes Maclean's deeper strains. Redford tries to maintain an even surface – one befitting this family's unruffled sense of decency – but to do so he refrains from such diversions as dramatic conflict and character development. The movie nearly dies from understatement. And it's hard to accept Brad Pitt as a brightly burning light when all he does is simulate Redford's smile and acting style. Even the central "river of life" metaphor fails to gather momentum. Ultimately, *A River Runs Through It* works best as a picture-book look at Montana's natural wonders. ~*Lawrence Frascella*

KaLIFOrnia

Rolling Stone, *September 16, 1993*

THIS KINKY GAME OF MURDER and eroticism is preposterous but never boring. Director Dominic Sena switches from music videos (Sting, David Bowie) to films and shows a keen eye for images that fill a wide screen with beauty and terror. Then the inconsistencies in Tim Metcalfe's script break the spell. But there is that cast – young, hot and acting for keeps. Juliette Lewis can test your

endurance with her insistent drawl and then use it to pierce your heart; she's flat-out wonderful as Adele Corners, a waitress who takes an innocent delight in trying on high heels her ex-con boyfriend Early Grayce (Brad Pitt) has stolen for her. The shoes are still warm from the feet of Early's latest victim, but, shucks, Adele doesn't know he's a serial killer.

Brian Kessler, played by David Duchovny, doesn't know, either. But he's writing a book on serial killers, and his girlfriend, Carrie (the gorgeous Michelle Forbes), is taking the photos. Since the plan is to drive cross-country to California visiting murder sites, Brian advertises for a couple to share expenses on the trip.

Why do these two sophisticates pick trailer trash like Adele and Early as travel mates? Don't look for logic – it's the quartet of actors that keeps you riveted. Pitt is outstanding, all boyish charm and then a snort that exudes pure menace. He and Lewis, once lovers offscreen, play this flapdoodle with enough urgency to make the suspension of disbelief worthwhile. ~*Peter Travers*

True romance

Rolling Stone, *September 30, 1993*

WHEN QUENTIN TARANTINO made his debut last year as the writer and director of *Reservoir Dogs,* there was no question that a rabid new talent had arrived to bite the ass of conventional filmmaking. Tarantino's movie-obsessed take on the world is the driving force behind *True Romance,* the savagely funny thrill ride based on the first script this former video-store clerk ever wrote. As Clarence Worley, Christian Slater plays a kung-fu and Elvis worshiper much like Tarantino. No sooner does he meet Alabama Whitman (Patricia Arquette) than Clarence is proposing marriage and defending her honor against her dreadlocked, drug-crazed, mob-connected former boyfriend Drexl Spivey, played by Gary Oldman as if there was no such thing as overacting.

Soon the newlyweds are fleeing Detroit for Los Angeles to sell Drexl's cocaine to Hollywood types, acted with spectacular sleaze by Saul Rubinek and Bronson Pinchot. But first the couple stops to say good-bye to Clarence's security-cop dad, Clifford (Dennis Hopper), who later runs into trouble with mob hit man Vicente Coccotti (Christopher Walken). The blistering confrontation scene between Hopper and Walken – both in peak form – will be talked about for years. It's pure Tarantino: a full-throttle blast of bloody action and verbal fireworks.

If the rest of *True Romance* never quite hits those heights of hothouse theatricality, maybe it's because some fool forgot to hire Tarantino to direct his own script. It's baffling why the plum fell to Tony Scott, the Britisher known for slick commercials and such megaton star vehicles as *Top Gun* and *Beverly Hills Cop II.* It's like pissing away your money for ripped jeans with a designer label. But the true grunge of the script wins out. And even Scott can't neuter the performances. Slater is terrific, reminding us of the vigorous promise he showed before sinking in the shallows of *Kuffs* and *Mobsters.* And Arquette delivers sensationally, especially in a vivid scene in which she gives a ballistic thrashing to the hood who's just beaten the bejesus out of her. Arquette and Slater make a wildly comic and sexy pair of bruised romantics. Everyone shines, right down to the smallest bits from Brad Pitt as a stoned innocent to Val Kilmer as the ghost of Elvis. But it's Tarantino's gutter poetry that detonates *True Romance.* This movie is dynamite.   ~*Peter Travers*

Interview with the vampire

Rolling Stone, *December 15, 1994*

NEIL JORDAN'S $50 MILLION FILM of Anne Rice's best-selling *Interview With the Vampire* is a major movie with major problems. Is it still worth seeing? Definitely. The good parts are that good. But it's one thing to write it in a review and another to say it in person to a potential ticket buyer who's in your face and wanting proof. Around this office, *Interview* really pushes people's buttons. They resent the unremitting hype, the glib cruelty of the genre and the casting of Tom Cruise as the blond, Byronic vampire Lestat (Rice resented it, too, but later recanted). The following "Interview With the Critic" will give you an idea of the hell raised when I recommended *Interview* to friends who can answer back.

Name one good thing about this movie.
I'll name five. The movie is hypnotic, scary, sexy, perversely funny and haunting in a way that taps into primal fears.
Get to the downside.
It can also be gross, snail paced and grindingly glum. You could say the same things – pro and con – about Rice's book.
What do you mean by "gross"?
Early on, Cruise slits the throat of a squirming rat, lets its blood drip into a wineglass and offers it to Brad Pitt, who plays vampire in training, with a warning to drink up before it gets cold.
So you're an expert on Rice?
I read her book, okay? And the followup *The Vampire Lestat* – the second of four books in her *Vampire Chronicles.* We're not talking great literature, but the book is more than a guilty pleasure.
Hasn't Rice compared Lestat to Captain Ahab, Custer and Peter the Great?
Yes, but she's kidding herself.
But you still think 'Interview' is strong material for a movie?
Damn straight. The plot pulls you in as soon as Lestat puts the bite on Louis de Pointe du Lac – that's Brad Pitt. He's a Louisiana plantation owner. Lestat was once a French aristocrat. He turns Louis into a vampire – there's an exchange of bodily fluids – because he likes pretty company and needs a nice place to stay. Louis regrets losing his humanity, and he and Lestat bicker for about two hundred years.
That sounds dull.
Well, it is repetitive. The bodies pile up. Jordan has moved from *The Crying Game* to *The Dying Game.* New Orleans burns. Louis finds more vampires in Paris – Stephen Rea plays a dangerous one, Antonio Banderas plays a dangerously sexy one. Louis plots to kill Lestat, and they both end up in 1994 New Orleans and San Francisco, where Louis gets interviewed by a reporter, well played by Christian Slater, and Lestat gets hooked by his first earful of rock – Guns n' Roses sing the Stones.
But Cruise as a worldly aristocrat? Come on.
No argument. Daniel Day-Lewis – with his sensual, tor-

mented face – was the perfect choice, but he turned down the part. Give Cruise credit for guts. It's an audacious performance. He broke ranks with the bland before – *Risky Business, Rain Man* and *Born on the Fourth of July* – but *Interview* is a real bust-out. Any star willing to kill women, children and pets onscreen is not that worried about protecting his image. Besides, Cruise's frat-boy charm fits in with Jordan's concept.
What concept is that?
Jordan loves jolts: the chick with a dick in *The Crying Game* and now Cruise hiding fangs behind his big grin. He's using Hollywood's young studs to play characters willing to trade their souls for eternal youth and beauty. It's a sly joke. And the actors don't have to fake competitiveness.
Does Pitt hold his ground against Cruise?
He has the tougher role. Louis is the story's conscience, and Pitt's expressive eyes reflect the inner turmoil. But Louis's whining against the dying of the light is not as riveting as Lestat's wicked rage against the machine.
Isn't there a gay angle?
The camera holds the orgasmic moment when Lestat first lifts Louis high in the air and bites into his throbbing artery. But vampires can't have sex. It's the kill that excites them, and that transcends gender.
What about love?
Louis and Lestat are inextricably linked. They even take a shot at being a family by creating a child vampire out of Claudia, a young orphan played by Kirsten Dunst. Claudia is the film's most unnerving character. She learns the art of flirting from Lestat, cuddles with Louis in his coffin and murders indiscriminately. "I want some more," says Claudia after her first taste of blood. It's a twist on *Oliver* that Dickens never imagined. As the decades pass, Claudia becomes a woman trapped in a child's body. It's a chilling portrait and a triumph for Dunst, who is twelve.
Why a kid vampire? What's the point?
Rice had a daughter named Michelle, who died of leukemia in 1972. During years of mourning in an alcoholic haze, Rice wrote *Interview With the Vampire* to help her deal with her grief and loss. The book was published in 1976.
So 'Interview' is cathartic for Rice?
For her and her legions of fans who read into the book their own personal stories. Some equate vampirism with alcoholism, depression, sexuality, AIDS – you name it.

B
R
A
D

Isn't that a stretch?

Not really. Gothic fantasies have always lent themselves to metaphorical interpretation: Look at *Frankenstein.* To sell *Interview* as escapism is to sell it short.

But that's just what Cruise and Jordan are saying in the press — that it's a vampire movie.

Can you blame them? Metaphors are a stake in the heart at the box office.

What's wrong with a simple vampire movie?

They've been done, pardon the expression, to death. Rice used her life to give her fiction deeper meaning. It's the metaphors that give the film resonance.

Which metaphors, for instance?

Addiction, for one. The vampires are like the nomadic young junkies in Gus Van Sant's *Drugstore Cowboy,* hungry for their next fix and ready to lie, cheat, steal or kill to get it. Like Van Sant, Jordan gives the forbidden its rightful allure. The promise of immortality is some high.

What did Rice get that Jordan missed?

The pain of separation. In the book, Louis and Lestat leave behind friends and family. It's quite poignant. Jordan plunges right into darkness. Cinematographer Philippe Rousselot uses only lanterns to illuminate this shadow world. The dimness is oppressive, and when the sun appears near the end, we squint against its deadly rays like they do. It's a devastating effect that earns sympathy for the devils. But it's only part of their story.

What's the rest?

The fading of human feeling. That's Louis's tragedy and ours, too. You don't have to be a vampire to know what it's like to sell out. But for all its visionary brilliance, the movie version of *Interview* never lets us close enough to see ourselves in Louis. We're dazzled but unmoved.

What will you say if others say different?

Bite me. *~Peter Travers*

US, *September 1994*

DIRECTOR NEIL JORDAN *(The Crying Game)* says that the enormous amount of controversy surrounding *Interview With the Vampire* – the century-spanning epic tale of a dysfunctional vampire family starring Tom Cruise, Brad Pitt and Christian Slater – actually helped the cast and crew. First,

Anne Rice, who wrote the novel on which the film is based, complained that Cruise wasn't right for the part of the vampire Lestat. Then there were questions about the amount of homoeroticism in the script. Next, Slater came on to fill the role of the Interviewer, left empty when River Phoenix died last fall. "It was deeply unpleasant, but it had a strangely positive effect," says Jordan. "We ended up just cutting ourselves off from the world." About translating the deeply sensual elements of the story from page to screen, Jordan says: "These vampires don't have sex. Sexual drives become blood lust, so you can have these incredibly erotic scenes without having two actors up onscreen going at it, which always make me cringe."

Legends of the Fall

Rolling Stone, *January 26, 1995*

IS IT TO BE THE BABE or the bear for Brad Pitt? That is the question. At least it is in the gorgeous and goofy *Legends of the Fall,* a tasty chunk of pop escapism that will most likely hit pay dirt at the mall, where audiences take their movies like the buttered popcorn — in sweet, nutrient-free puffs that go down easy. As Tristan, the middle son of Montana rancher Colonel William Ludlow (Anthony Hopkins), Pitt must choose between the call of the nest in the form of a marriageable woman (Julia Ormond) and the call of the wild in the form of a pissed-off grizzly (Bart the bear) who tears his flesh and invades his soul. No contest. This is Jim Harrison country, where the macho ethic of the Michigan poet reigns supreme. Remember Harrison's *Wolf,* in which Jack Nicholson also got nipped by a furry mammal and turned primitive? Director Mike Nichols played the myth for laughs.

In *Legends,* director Edward Zwick plays the myth straight. Harrison is still waiting for a kindred spirit, say Oliver Stone, to capture his Gonzo poetry onscreen. Zwick is too slick for primal urges. He plays *Legends* for the ponderous sweep he brought to *Glory* and the glossy angst he patented as a creator of TV's *thirtysomething.* Susan Shilliday, who cowrote the *Legends* script with Bill Wittliff, also toiled on the yuppie whinefest. Whatever *Legends* is on film, it is not Harrison.

Zwick is aiming for a sprawling family saga in the tradition of *Giant.* And boy, does this badly sprawl. The story begins after the turn of the century, when the young Tristan first meets the bear, and ends with their final battle in 1963. The film is narrated by One Stab (Gordon Tootoosis), the Cree warrior who serves as a scout for William Ludlow and later as a hand on his Montana ranch. When the colonel's wife returns to her native Boston, One Stab helps the old man raise his three sons: ambitious Alfred (Aidan Quinn), naive Samuel (Henry Thomas – that's right: the *E.T.* kid all grown up) and untamed Tristan. One Stab introduces Tristan to American Indian ways, such as the joy of the kill, when a hunter cuts out the warm heart of an animal, "setting its spirit free."

In 1913, Samuel returns from Harvard to introduce his fiancée, Susannah (Ormond). "How intoxicating to have a cultivated woman in the house again," says the colonel. Indeed. Ormond, a London stage actress, is a radiant discovery. Alfred is drawn to Susannah, she to Tristan. These early scenes of divided loyalties and secret passions are the film's best.

Then tragedy strikes. And keeps striking. First, World War I. Even Tristan can't save Samuel on the battlefields of France; he can only cut out the dead boy's heart and – you guessed it – set his spirit free. While the globe-trotting Tristan works out his torment with sex and drugs, Susannah marries Alfred, now a congressman. The colonel suffers a stroke, driving Hopkins into spasms of giggle-inducing overacting. There is murder, accidental death, suicide – all set to an overblown score by James Horner. There is even a rematch for the bear and Tristan, who refuses to shoot his prey. One Stab knows why: "The old ones say when a man and an animal have spilled each other's blood, they become one."

The old ones have probably seen a lot of hokey movies. What makes *Legends* such an entertaining male weepie is the star shine. Though the admirable Quinn has the toughest role, Pitt carries the picture. The blue-eyed boy who seemed a bit lost in *Interview With the Vampire* proves himself a bona fide movie star, stealing every scene he's in. Face it: The babe and the bear never had a chance.   ~*Peter Travers*

BASED ON JIM HARRISON'S NOVELLA, *Legends of the Fall* is the epic, often schmaltzy, thoroughly enjoyable story of three very different sons (Aidan Quinn, Brad Pitt and Henry Thomas) raised by their father (Anthony Hopkins) in World War I–era Montana. British actress Julia Ormond makes an impressive American film debut as the woman who is loved by all three sons. Her chemistry with Pitt was helped along by the fact that the two shared a house on location – "as roommates, I hasten to say, not as lovers," says director Ed Zwick *(Glory).* All the performances in *Legends* are strong, but this is a star-making vehicle for Pitt. "It's undeniable," says Zwick. "His physicality – the riding and stunts – juxtaposed with his vulnerability succeed in painting a picture of a man who is a force of nature."

seven

Rolling Stone, *October 5, 1995*

BLAME THE CULTURAL IMPACT of Quentin Tarantino's *Pulp Fiction* for the current crime wave at the movies. This new age of renegade film noir is immune to Bob Dole's brimstone. You can't hit the cineplex these days without being loogied by blood spray and gobs of lurid dialogue.

An ambitious film that shows how crime fiction can go beyond bang-bang to give us new ways of thinking about the bad old world, *Seven* is a crime story that leans heavily on atmosphere. But this nerve-jangling thriller, evocatively shot by Darius Khondji, is no period piece. Set in an unnamed modern city deluged by rain and eroded by decay, the film stars Brad Pitt as David Mills, a can-do detective just in from the sticks with his wife, Tracy (Gwyneth Paltrow), to replace Lieutenant William Somerset (Morgan Freeman), a soul-sick cop ready to pack it in after thirty-four years of chasing scumbags.

The case that brings the two together is a John Doe serial killer who bases his murders on the seven deadly sins. For gluttony, a fatso is forced to eat until he bursts. For pride, a model is brutally disfigured. And so on through greed, sloth and lust. Envy and wrath are paired for a twisted, gut-wrenching climax.

Andrew Kevin Walker wrote the script while working at Tower Records in Manhattan. But don't take this skin-crawler of a mood piece for pulp escapism. Pitt drops the movie-star glamour as a stubbly hothead. Freeman, an actor of consummate subtlety, plays the cooler hand. They make a fine, fierce team. Only a dinner organized by Tracy (the gifted Paltrow is underused) takes the chill off the two cops. Later, Tracy confides in William why she's afraid to tell her husband she's pregnant. It's a rare nod to sentiment. Humor is also scarce, though Pitt's barely literate cop gets a big laugh when he pronounces the Marquis de Sade as "Shar-day."

Seven wants to abrade, not ingratiate. Director David Fincher got hammered for turning *Alien 3,* his feature debut, from a monster mash into an AIDS parable. That's what happens when you aim high in Hollywood: You're labeled pretentious. Fincher is not entirely blameless. Characters are sometimes merely attitudes posing as people. And the request that critics refrain from revealing who plays John Doe (okay, I won't tell, but it's a superactor, not a superstar) smacks of gimmickry. It's not the identity of the killer that gives *Seven* its kick — it's the way Fincher raises mystery to the level of moral provocation. If *Pulp Fiction* has given us a taste for such challenge, then we have Tarantino to thank instead of blame.   *~Peter Travers*

12 MONKEYS

Rolling Stone, *January 25, 1996*

EVEN WHEN TERRY GILLIAM'S latest leap into the wild blue of futuristic fantasy is at its most confounding, you leap along with him. Such is the seductive power of his twisted imagination. Whether it's Monty Python, *Brazil, Time Bandits* or *The Fisher King,* Gilliam guarantees a thrilling ride. *12 Monkeys* is no exception. Bruce Willis, in an eruptive performance of startling emotional intensity, stars as Cole, a prisoner tagged for an experiment that may get him killed.

The year is 2035. Nearly forty years earlier, a killer virus spared only 1 percent of the planet's population. In a lab located under the city of Philadelphia, scientists prepare to wrap the naked Cole in condomlike latex and zap him back to 1996 to find out how to reclaim the earth. Above ground the city is uninhabitable, except by the wild animals who roam deserted skyscrapers and department stores. Gilliam, along with the gifted cinematographer Roger Pratt and production designer Jeffrey Beecroft, fashions a disturbing and dazzling lost world.

Credit is also due to screenwriters David Peoples (*Unforgiven, Blade Runner)* and his wife, Janet, who took Chris Marker's evocative 1962 short film *La Jetée* and enriched it with their own stirring vision of a future haunted by the past. When Cole travels back in time, he is immediately institutionalized and put in the care of psychiatrist Kathryn Railly (Madeleine Stowe). Cole is befriended by a patient, Jeffrey Goines (Brad Pitt), an animal-rights activist and the nut-job son of a medical researcher (Christopher Plummer) whose virus experiments on lab creatures drive Jeffrey into a foaming frenzy. Pitt is terrific, finding a mad fire in a character that is miles from movie-star glamour.

Through Jeffrey, Cole first learns about the army of the 12 Monkeys. It would be unfair to give away more, except to say that the plot kicks in when Cole kidnaps Kathryn, played by the gorgeous Stowe with fierce intelligence and a passionate heart. Her growing belief in a man who doesn't trust his own sanity sparks an unexpectedly moving love story. Cole is haunted by a recurring dream of a young boy at an airport. The boy stands transfixed as a man with a suitcase rushes past him, followed by a blond woman who weeps by the man's side after the police gun him down. The tenderness of the woman as she kisses the dying man's bloody hand deeply affects Cole and the boy.

This dream is the soul of the film. Gilliam returns to it three times, adding more details until the dream links all the pieces in the puzzle, which includes the remarkable David Morse as a researcher with more than a passing interest in Kathryn. Cole's confusing of illusion and reality suggests Alfred Hitchcock's masterwork *Vertigo,* in which a mentally unbalanced James Stewart tries to turn Kim Novak into a reincarnation of the woman he loves, who has died. Cole and

Kathryn hide in a movie-revival house showing *Vertigo*. The 1958 film, now yellowed with age, shows Novak in the Muir Woods using her finger to trace the small space on the rings of a cut redwood that encompasses the years of her life. Bernard Herrmann's haunting *Vertigo* score plays over the dialogue between Cole and Kathryn as they leave the theater in an attempt to carve out their own small space in life. Rarely has one film referenced another with such poetic grace. Like *Vertigo, 12 Monkeys* rewards multiple viewings. You might say it even demands them. For all the fun, fright and hypnotic romance that Gilliam delivers, he digs deepest into fatalistic themes that usually scare away the crowds at the box office. Go with Gilliam anyway. Solving the riddle of *12 Monkeys* is an exhilarating challenge.   *~Peter Travers*

US, *December 1995*

THE MOVIE '12 MONKEYS' puts a sci-fi spin on Hollywood's latest craze: deadly viruses. Bruce Willis stars as a Twenty-first-Century prisoner sent back to 1996 to find the source of a disease that has almost wiped out humanity. Madeleine Stowe is his doubting shrink, and Brad Pitt plays an animal-rights psychopath who's part of the puzzle. "The killer virus has replaced the atomic bomb as America's obsession," says director Terry Gilliam *(The Fisher King)*. "We're taking total advantage of that."

SLeePers

Rolling Stone, *October 31, 1996*

ISN'T 'SLEEPERS' THE NONFICTION BOOK that critics tried to shoot down as a sham after author Lorenzo Carcaterra sold his 1995 memoir to Hollywood for a cool $2 million? You got that right. Now the powerfully unsettling movie version is under fire. Despite the hot cast – young contenders Brad Pitt and Jason Patric mixing it up with heavyweights Robert De Niro and Dustin Hoffman – the heartfelt direction of Barry Levinson *(Rain Man)* and Carcaterra's true-crime story, *Sleepers* (the street name for boys who do time in a juvenile facility) still invites suspicion.

Carcaterra isn't fazed. He admits that he changed names, dates and some locations to protect the identities of those involved. Otherwise, *Sleepers* is his life as one of four Catholic schoolboys who were raised in New York's Hell's Kitchen area in the 1960s, remanded to reform school after a prank with a hot-dog cart nearly killed an old man, raped and brutalized by school guards, and reunited as adults in a revenge plot that ends in murder and a coverup.

Hard to swallow? Levinson says that Carcaterra's vivid storytelling supersedes questions of exact authenticity, even an implausible trial scene. When assistant district attorney Michael Sullivan (Pitt) prosecutes John Reilly (Ron Eldard) and Tommy Marcano (Billy Crudup) for shooting security guard Sean Nokes (Kevin Bacon), the killers feel betrayed. Michael was their friend in Hell's Kitchen. So was Lorenzo Carcaterra (Patric), the aspiring reporter. All endured the same abuse from Nokes in reform school. That's where bookworm Lorenzo, known as Shakes (for Shakespeare), gave his pals a taste for the sweet revenge he read about in *The Count of Monte Cristo.* "I'm not taking the case to win," says Michael, to Shakes's relief. "I'm taking it to lose."

With the help of gangster King Benny (Vittorio Gassman) and childhood pal Carol (an underused Minnie Driver), the sleepers have their vengeance. They bring in defense lawyer Danny Snyder (Dustin Hoffman in sly comic form), a drunk who can be trusted to keep quiet about the fix. The chief defense witness is Father Bobby (De Niro), the neighborhood priest who perjures himself by swearing he was with John and Tommy on the night of the murder.

Since objections from the Catholic Church and the Manhattan district attorney's office (no murder trial resembling this one is on the books) have failed to persuade Carcaterra to reveal his sources, the film relies on the emotional candor of the actors to make believers of us all. Pitt and Patric offer unflinching glimpses into haunted men. In less-defined roles, Eldard and Crudup also excel. The sleepers can't discuss the year inside that they spent with Nokes, even with each other. When Shakes finally opens up to Father Bobby, Levinson lets us read the horror on the priest's face in a harrowing close-up that De Niro renders with indelible impact.

Unlike *The Boys of St. Vincent, Sleepers* offers no insights into the torment of men like Nokes. The film's concern is one for the abused boys, superbly played by Brad Renfro (Michael), Joe

Perrino (Shakes), Geoffrey Wigdor (John) and Jonathan Tucker (Tommy), who rightly dominate the film's first hour. As in *Diner* and *Avalon,* Levinson shows a keen eye for the pangs of adolescence. Michael Ballhaus's luminous cinematography polishes those days of talking sex and playing stickball until Hell's Kitchen shines like a concrete Camelot. Idealized? You bet. That's why the loss of this world must be avenged with the same broad strokes that you'd expect from the Count of Monte Cristo.

"We lived inside every book we read, every movie we saw," Carcaterra wrote. "We were Cagney in *Angels With Dirty Faces.* . . . We were Ivanhoe on our own city streets." These words are the key to *Sleepers'* vaultingly romantic style and its core truth. No one challenges Carcaterra's previous nonfiction book, *A Safe Place,* in which he learns, at fourteen, that his father had served time for killing his first wife. It's public record. *Sleepers,* for all the doubts it raises, is the work of a man who speaks for absent friends and "for the children we were." It's his secret heart. Leave the matter of getting away with murder to Carcaterra and his conscience. Onscreen, in the faces of these lost children, the pain is real.   ~*Peter Travers*

THE DEVIL'S OWN

Rolling Stone, *April 17, 1997*

HAVE YOU NOTICED? Bad dudes don't want to stay bad anymore. In *The Saint,* Val Kilmer's Simon Templar — the playboy prince of thieves — is reformed by the love of a good woman physicist (Elisabeth Shue). In *The Devil's Own,* Brad Pitt's Frankie "the Angel" McGuire — an IRA terrorist, dangerous in battle and bed — is taught the art of nonviolence by a fatherly New York cop (Harrison Ford) who unknowingly shelters a killer. Need more excuses to root for these fugitives? Both films show the hero being traumatized in childhood by watching a loved one die violently.

Get out your handkerchiefs. Or better yet, your calendars. It's barely spring, yet Hollywood is pretending it's summer. *The Saint,* a $68 million action epic shot in Moscow and London, sure sounds like hot-weather escapism to me. Ditto *The Devil's Own,* a $90 million thriller shot in Dublin and New York. Clashing egos, ballooning budgets and re-shot

endings plagued both of these movies. You hear that a lot in summer, the season when studios and stars care more about crowd pleasing than creativity.

The Devil's Own, which centers on the conflict between Pitt's Belfast terrorist and Ford's Staten Island cop, gets off to a scrappy start before director Alan J. Pakula *(Presumed Innocent)* lets it go soft. Pitt found the early stages of the film "irresponsible." Translation: When Ford agreed to play the police sergeant Tom O'Meara, the Kevin Jarre story that Pitt had signed on to do was rewritten by many hands. "We made it up as we went along," said Pitt.

It doesn't look that way. Despite the toxic buzz, *The Devil's Own* is a surprisingly coherent look at lawbreaking. The problem is, there are few other surprises outside of Pitt's one-of-the-lads brogue. You expect more than a plodding character study broken by bursts of violence.

The deck is stacked in the film's prologue as eight-year-old Frankie watches his father get gunned down at home. Frankie views his revenge against the British as a holy war. The film pretends not to take sides, but Pitt is its star and meal ticket.

Cinematographer Gordon Willis lights Pitt like an angel in blond hair and dark leather. Even Frankie's passport photo looks like the cover of *Hunk Beautiful.* It's the hunk the film's trailer is selling. Pitt's blue eyes gleam as he shoots the baddies, beds the babe and locks horns with Ford, who looks unduly glum (the *Star Wars* reissue has made us miss his light touch).

Pitt and Ford try to dig deeper, but the script undercuts them with preachy dialogue that might as well read, "Insert stereotype here." Frankie charms Tom's wife, Sheila (Margaret Colin), and their young daughters. He uses Tom's home as a cover to buy missiles from the lethal Billy Burke (Treat Williams). When Frankie's betrayal puts the O'Mearas in peril, Tom's rage rivals Frankie's guilt.

Ultimately, Frankie sees the good in Tom, a cop who abhors violence. Frankie sees his love for Megan (Natascha McElhone) reflected in Tom's love for Sheila. Mostly he sees Tom as the father he lost. It's hokey, but Pitt and Ford act with feeling until the bloody climax, when you damn near choke on the male bonding and noble sacrifice. In its rush to show that there's no such thing as a bad boy if the boy is a movie star, Hollywood has taken the devilish fun out of escapism. The sanitized do-gooders of *The Devil's Own* leave you begging for these guys to go and sin some more.   ~*Peter Travers* ◻

(1) BRAD PITT SEDUCES GEENA DAVIS IN 'THELMA & LOUISE'; (2) PITT AS A RICKY NELSON WANNABE IN 'JOHNNY SUEDE'; (3) PITT WITH AN ANIMATED COSTAR IN 'COOL WORLD'; (4) PITT AS FLY-FISHERMAN PAUL MACLEAN IN 'A RIVER RUNS THROUGH IT'; (5) PITT AS EARLY GRAYCE AND JULIETTE LEWIS AS ADELE CORNERS IN 'KALIFORNIA'; (6) PITT AS THE POTHEAD ROOMMATE IN 'TRUE ROMANCE'; (7) PITT AS VAMPIRE INDUCTEE LOUIS IN 'INTERVIEW WITH THE VAMPIRE'

A BRAD PITT FILMOGRAPHY

{ BY PETER TRAVERS }

NO ACTOR THROWS HOLLYWOOD more curveballs than Brad Pitt. Once the studio moneymen think they have him pegged as a movie star who is less interested in quality work than picking up $10 million for such action escapism as *The Devil's Own,* Pitt brings the glamour down and signs up for a film that no studio would dare make if Pitt wasn't in it. At this writing, the thirty-three-year-old phenom is about to open in *Seven Years in Tibet,* a World War II period piece in which he plays Austrian mountain climber Heinrich Harrer. Based on Harrer's book of the same name, the film – directed by Frenchman Jean-Jacques Annaud – details how Harrer escaped from an Allied prison camp in India, made his way to Tibet, and wound up teaching the art of mountain climbing and other matters philosophical to a kid who happened to be the Dalai Lama. Hardly manna for a box office that feeds on Jim Carrey comedies and sequels to screen fantasies about dinosaurs, aliens, speed freaks and batmen.

Pitt gets away with it. His popularity is at its peak, except in China where the government still holds a grudge against the Dalai Lama and barred filming of *Seven Years in Tibet.* Pitt and company moved on to India until pressure was also brought to bear there. They settled in Argentina, where the Andes could be made to look like the Himalayas and Pitt could put on his mountain gear and start climbing. (The Canadian Rockies were used, too.) Even when bearded and bedraggled, Pitt cuts a star figure as Harrer. The jury is still out on whether Pitt can draw a large audience to a film about mountain climbing, a subject that has spawned dozens of flops (Remember *K2*? No? My point exactly) and even left Clint Eastwood *(The Eiger Sanction)* dangling from the ropes. And if this foray into Tibetan mysticism and the metaphorical implications of scaling mountains doesn't make a dime, that's not Pitt's concern. Hollywood may see this golden boy as star insurance, but he defines himself differently.

Pitt claims he's an actor. Those words usually get a laugh when spoken by someone whose looks are suitable for framing. Still, a close examination of Pitt's career indicates that the golden boy is right. At first, Pitt wasn't fussy about what kind of jobs he took when he dropped out of the University of Missouri shortly before graduation and headed for Hollywood. Blink and you'll miss him in *Less Than Zero* (1987). Don't even try to watch *Cutting Class* (1989), a high school slasher flick, or *Happy Together* (1989), a college comedy. He fared marginally better on television with roles in soaps – daytime *(Another World)* and nighttime *(Dallas)* – though his big shot at series stardom, *Glory Days,* was mercifully canceled after a few episodes. *Too Young to Die,* a 1990 TV movie he did with his soon-to-be-girlfriend Juliette Lewis, gave the first inkling of promise.

Then came the breakthrough year – 1991. *Across the Tracks* cast Pitt as the track-star brother of bad boy Rick Schroder. Pitt should have had Schroder's role as the reform-school troublemaker. Stuck instead with the straight-arrow role, he played it without an ounce of "I'm better than this" condescension. Pitt was credible and moving. Nobody saw the movie; they didn't need to. Opening that same year was *Thelma & Louise,* the critical and box-office smash that many people, including Pitt, like to think of as his movie debut.

You can see why. In a role that limits Pitt to less than fifteen minutes of screen time, he is extraordinary. Pitt plays J.D., a hitchhiking stud in cowboy boots that the feminist outlaws Thelma (Geena Davis) and Louise (Susan Sarandon), who were just a housewife and a waitress when they started out, pick up on their getaway ride to Mexico. Director Ridley Scott's first shot of Pitt sets him off like another J.D., the young James Dean in *Giant,* with his hat and posture sporting a rakish tilt. Thelma, panting like a puppy, begs Louise to

stop and pick him up. For their trouble, the ladies are treated to a dose of J.D. charm. "Miss Thelma," he drawls, "how is it you haven't got any kids? I mean, God gives you something special, I think you ought to pass it on." Even the uptight Louise is won over when J.D. drops the polite act to say that Thelma's husband "sounds like a real asshole."

Pitt is in first-class company here, working with a stylish director, an Oscar-winning script by Callie Khouri and two potent actresses in peak form. But Pitt pulls off his big scene, shirtless in a motel bed with Davis, with an uncommon display of talent, energy, humor and physical grace. J.D. is confessing to Thelma that he robs convenience stores. Picking up her hair dryer and sticking it in his jeans, he gives a demonstration while standing in bed. "Ladies and gentlemen," says J.D., pulling out his weapon, "let's see who can win the prize for keepin' their cool. Simon says everybody down on the floor, now. Nobody loses their head, then nobody loses their head." J.D. stops to drink in Thelma's appreciation of his little joke and gentlemanly behavior. "I've always believed that if done properly, armed robbery doesn't have to be a totally unpleasant experience."

Thelma is shocked but impressed at this real live outlaw. "I may be an outlaw, darlin'," says J.D., "but you're the one stealin' my heart." J.D. will end by stealing all the money Thelma and Louise have, but not before he and Thelma indulge in a bout of room-trashing, body-bashing sex that she never got at home.

In a movie about male betrayal, J.D. is one more example. Yet Pitt allows the character a share of wayward decency. Captured by the police, J.D. runs into Thelma's fool husband at the station and goads him into a fight. J.D. felt a bond with Thelma that the audience feels as well. Director Scott salutes him with a shot, viewed through a car's rearview mirror. It's J.D., on the road alone in the rain, doing a little two-step. Brad Pitt became a star in that scene, and an actor, too.

The new star dimmed considerably the next year in Ralph Bakshi's *Cool World,* an unsavory mix of live action and animation that tried and failed to imitate the success of the 1988 Steven Spielberg/Disney hit *Who Framed Roger Rabbit.* Pitt, as detective Frank Harris, is zapped into a cartoon world of violence and sex, the latter represented by a blond bombshell named Holli Wood (voiced by Kim Basinger). Holli longs to get it on with a human, namely Jack Deebs (Gabriel Byrne), the cartoonist who drew her. Humans having sex with doodles is against the law, and Frank has sworn to enforce it despite his own relationship with a hot package of ink-drawn

curves named Lonette. "It's frustrating," Frank moans. "I'm like a plug without a socket."

If that raunchy dialogue isn't embarrassing enough, wait until you see Pitt try to act with a blue screen (the cartoon characters are added later). Bob Hoskins pulled it off in *Roger Rabbit,* but *Cool World* is so technically clumsy that Pitt appears to be staring off into space. Still, his tough-guy banter with Byrne hints at the teasing Pitt will take for his looks in the years ahead. "I'm not one of your creations!" Pitt's detective yells to Byrne's cartoonist. "No, you're not pretty enough," counters Jack, adding a snide remark about Frank's perfectly blow-dried locks: "Where'd you get your hair done?"

Pitt's hair rises to new heights in Tom DiCillo's *Johnny Suede,* a playfully hip fantasy in which the actor plays a wannabe pop singer who models himself on Ricky Nelson and sports a pompadour that won't quit. Johnny is a musician who fancies himself as something better than he is. If he needs to borrow a hairstyle or a pair of blue suede shoes to be a star, he'll do it. Pitt's performance is nicely low-key, as is the movie. It's interesting to compare *Johnny Suede* with DiCillo's 1995 film *Living in Oblivion,* a hilarious satire of independent filmmaking in which James LeGros plays an egomaniac Hollywood actor who insiders say is a parody of the movie star Pitt became. DiCillo has denied such an intent, but the fact that LeGros's character is called Chad Palomino – please note that Chad rhymes with Brad and both last names begin with a "P" – suggests otherwise. In one scene, Chad/Brad notices a cameraman named Wolf (Dermot Mulroney) is wearing an eyepatch. Chad thinks it's cool, so he starts wearing one, too, although there is nothing wrong with Chad's eye. Chad looks to Wolf for approval but gets only a remark of "Kiss my ass" from the camera ace.

Despite the disappointments of *Johnny Suede* and *Cool World,* Pitt found another 1992 movie to turn the tide of his career. In Robert Redford's *A River Runs Through It,* a gentle tale of two Montana brothers who share a love of fly-fishing, Pitt's boyish good looks hurled him to stardom. Craig Sheffer played Norman Maclean, the quiet, scholarly brother. Not surprisingly, Pitt played Paul Maclean, the wild one. Both brothers compete for the affection of their stoic father (Tom Skerritt), a Presbyterian minister who cannot articulate his feelings for his wife, played by Brenda Blethyn of *Secrets and Lies,* or his two sons. For attention, Paul shoots the Montana rapids at night, gambles, drinks, fights, gets involved with an Indian woman. Redford narrates the film in the voice of Norman, but it's Paul who is the film's main focus. Norman speaks of fly-fishing as a metaphor for growing up and of how his brother turned casting for trout into an art, something even the preacher admired. Critics talked about how much Pitt looked like the young Redford. Teenage girls who couldn't care less about fly-fishing suddenly rushed to see a movie on the subject. The quiet dignity of Pitt's performance lost amid the star-making machinery merits a repeat viewing now on video. "Maybe all I really know about Paul is that he was a fine fisherman," says Norman after Paul's funeral. Paul had been beaten to death with the butt of a revolver, his body dumped in an alley. For once, his father is not silent. "You know more than that," says the old man, finding words at last. "He was beautiful." The last shot of Pitt is of his face, the sun smiling on his golden hair as he holds a prize catch. There was no way Pitt could avoid the star trap now.

Maybe not, but credit Pitt for trying. In 1993 he uglied up to star in Dominic Sena's *Kalifornia,* one of those grungy indie flicks geared to turn off little girls who tape Brad Pitt posters to their walls. As Early Grayce, a bearded, snorting piece of trailer trash who also happens to be a serial killer, Pitt is nearly unrecognizable. The movie was generally dissed by critics who recognized its pretensions but mostly failed to recognize how deeply Pitt dug into the role. Shacked up with Adele, a childish waitress indelibly played by Juliette Lewis, Early swills beer at breakfast, beats Adele, murders his landlord, runs out on his parole officer and hooks up himself and Adele on a car trip to California with a writer (David Duchovny) and his photographer girlfriend (Michelle Forbes) who are doing a book on — are you ready for this? — serial killers. Pitt is genuinely terrifying in this role. It's a seductively malevolent performance. His scenes with Duchovny take on a special resonance now that Duchovny is starring in *The X-Files.* It's Early who seems ready for a guest spot on that smash TV series. He keeps seeing doors on the side of the road, doors with "lights comin' out blindin' me." Before Early starts racking up the body count, he takes time out to teach the writer about the manly art of guns. "Gotta hold it soft like your pecker," he advises.

Tony Scott's *True Romance,* with a script by Quentin Tarantino, is another 1993 film in which Pitt is cast against type. His role is little more than a cameo. Pitt merely lies around on a filthy couch in an L.A. apartment, getting stoned and watching the Emilio Estevez sci-fi flick *Freejack* on TV as the *True Romance* characters come and go asking directions.

"They were here, and they said that they were going to go there, and they went." Pitt's stoner is invariably friendly even to the bad guys. "Oh, man. You guys want to smoke a bowl?" Even in a bit part, Pitt shows a comic flair that should be further developed.

Not, unfortunately, in Donald Petrie's *The Favor,* in which Pitt plays a hapless pawn. A married woman (Harley Jane Kozak) asks her single friend (Elizabeth McGovern) to sleep with an old boyfriend she never got around to in high school. Pitt, in a suit yet, looks understandably uncomfortable. Released in 1994, *The Favor* was made in 1991 when Pitt was in his eager-for-any-job phase. It's a career nadir.

Pitt recouped nicely in 1994 with two box-office hits: Neil Jordan's *Interview With the Vampire,* costarring Tom Cruise, and Edward Zwick's *Legends of the Fall,* with lots of closeups of Pitt's long, flowing hair. *Interview,* based on the Anne Rice bestseller, is by far the best bet. At the time so much attention was focused on Pitt and Cruise playing blood-sucking ghouls that little attention was paid to acting. A second viewing reveals that Pitt is astonishingly good as Louis, the twenty-four-year-old Louisiana plantation owner who is bitten by Cruise's vampire Lestat and banished to the darkness. "I haven't been human for two hundred years," Louis tells the San Francisco reporter (played by Christian Slater) who interviews him in New Orleans in the present. Pitt's scenes with Slater have a lightness of touch that the rest of the film lacks. Louis seems to enjoy freaking out the interviewer with his swift, powerful movements and his refusal to be bothered by stakes and crucifixes. Responding to the reporter's comment "I thought vampires didn't like the light," Louis says, "We love it," letting an overhead bulb illuminate the blue veins under his pale skin. Pitt underplays Louis's power beautifully until he unleashes his revenge on Lestat.

Pitt looks a lot livelier in *Legends,* as Tristan, the son of a Montana rancher (a scenery-chewing Anthony Hopkins). Tristan is drawn to bears (don't ask) and the wife (Julia Ormond) of his brother, played by Aidan Quinn. It's soap opera shot through with bits of the poetic mysticism you find better realized in Jim Harrison's novella. But Pitt puts on quite a display of movie-star fireworks. Can it be an accident that Philippe Rousselot, who shot *A River Runs Through It,* and John Toll, who shot *Legends,* both won Oscars for cinematography? Look at their subject. And I'm not just talking Montana.

The feeling persists that Pitt is uneasy with films that show him off like a prize stud. In 1995 he played it tough and driven as detective David Mills in David Fincher's *Seven.* It's a tribute to Fincher's memorable ferocity that *Seven* is remembered as much more than the film on which Pitt began his relationship with Gwyneth Paltrow, who plays David's pregnant wife Tracy. She calls him Serpico, and David has that same hotheaded drive. Pitt's the new cop in town, reporting to Lieutenant William Somerset (the great Morgan Freeman) on the case of a serial killer who bases his crimes on the seven deadly sins. "It would be great for me if we didn't start out kicking each other in the balls," David tells his fellow cop. The excellent cast includes Kevin Spacey as a killer wicked mad enough to send David his wife's severed head in a box. It's hardly the ending to spark a romance, but Pitt and Paltrow – whose real-life engagement was short-lived – can take justifiable pride in what they accomplish in *Seven.*

At the end of 1995, Pitt broke convention again and appeared in a supporting role in Terry Gilliam's *12 Monkeys.* Stars aren't supposed to stoop. Oh, yeah? Pitt won an Oscar nomination as Best Supporting Actor (and a Golden Globe award) for his role as Jeffrey Goines, an animal activist whom Bruce Willis, as a time-traveling convict named Cole, meets in a mental hospital. Pitt is first seen cowering in a chair, twitching, biting his fingernails and hiding his head under his shirt. No trace here of the star of *Legends of the Fall.* Jeffrey speaks in rapid-fire bursts – like the mentally challenged pianist Oscar-winner Geoffrey Rush played in *Shine* – but Pitt finds the sense behind the seeming gibberish. "There's the television," he tells Cole, indicating the box the patients watch with drugged inattention. "Look, listen, kneel, pray. We're consumers. Okay, *okay,* buy a lot of stuff and you're a good citizen. But if you don't buy a lot of stuff, what are you then, I ask you? Mentally ill!" There is a palpable excitement in watching Pitt engaged with challenging material.

Pitt didn't find a role as worthy in Barry Levinson's *Sleepers,* the 1996 film version of Lorenzo Carcaterra's novel about four Catholic boys who take revenge in adulthood for crimes committed against them in reform school. Pitt plays Michael Sullivan, one of those boys and now the assistant district attorney who rigs a murder case in favor of his friends. Though Pitt invests Michael with enormous sympathy, the role is severely underwritten. You can't blame Pitt for signing on anyway, since *Sleepers* gave him the chance to work with veterans Robert De Niro and Dustin Hoffman in scenes that remain the film's highlights.

Pitt found more script problems in 1996 with Alan J. Pakula's *The Devil's Own.* He complained publicly of the "irresponsibility" of shooting a film before a script was ready, claiming that he tried to drop out of the film until the studio head told him he would be held liable for $63 million in costs. Having seen the finished film, Pitt is less harsh. Yet his performance as IRA terrorist Frankie "the Angel" McGuire never blends satisfactorily with that of his costar Harrison Ford, playing Tom O'Meara, the New York cop Frankie uses as a cover to buy weapons for his cause. Aside from a credible Belfast accent, Pitt rarely gets to push his range. The film has him strike poses as a blond killer in black leather. The dramatic sparks remain unstruck.

Seven Years in Tibet finds Pitt in more comfortable dramatic territory in the kind of role he likes: adventurer. If Pitt is going to continue his adventure as an actor, he needs to fight the pressures Hollywood lays on stars to conform and sell tickets. It's fascinating to go back to *Interview With the Vampire* and tease out a subtext that doesn't involve vampires at all. There's Tom Cruise, a major star, inducting newcomer Brad Pitt into the ranks. Cruise's first bite gives Pitt a taste of the heavens – they literally shoot up into the skies. "What if I could give it back to you? Pluck out the pain and give you another life, one you could never imagine?" asks Cruise. "You can be young always, my friend, as we are now." Sounds good, huh? And movies do offer a kind of immortality. Centuries after Cruise's induction, Pitt is seen visiting a movie theater. Of course, there is also the trap. Vampires [read: stars] can't lead normal lives. They're doomed to stay hidden from the real world and repeat the same patterns that made them vampires [read: stars] in the first place. Then there's the competition factor. When Pitt reduces Cruise to a decrepit wreck, he pays a visit to gloat. After commenting on Pitt's "beauty," Cruise begs to relive the past. "You remember how I was, the vampire [read: star] that I was?" Of course, Cruise rallies in the end to put the bite on Christian Slater. Christian, are you listening?

It's not a pretty picture. Trust Pitt to resist giving up his real life for a Hollywood existence. The kid from Missouri is too much of a rebel to let other people choose his movies or live his life. Look at his next film, Martin Brest's *Meet Joe Black* – Pitt plays someone who falls in love and takes a holiday. Sounds conventional, except that Pitt is playing Death taking a day off from his duties as the Grim Reaper. Pitt's trip from *Thelma & Louise* to *Seven,* from mainstream movies to independents and back again, proves that as much as he grows as an actor, he'll stay a hardnose forever. ◻

THE MOVIES

No Man's Land *(1985)*
Director: Alain Tanner
Character: extra

Less Than Zero *(1987)*
Director: Marek Kanievska
Character: extra

A Stoning in Fulham County
(1988, television)
Director: Larry Elikman
Character: Teddy Johnson

Cutting Class *(1989, television)*
Director: Rospo Pallenberg
Character: Dwight

Happy Together *(1989, television)*
Director: Mel Damski
Character: Brian

The Image *(1989, television)*
Director: Peter Werner
Character: Steve Black

Too Young to Die? *(1990, television)*
Director: Robert Markowitz
Character: Billy Canton

Across the Tracks *(1991, television)*
Director: Sandy Tung
Character: Joe Maloney

Thelma & Louise *(1991)*
Director: Ridley Scott
Character: J.D.

Johnny Suede *(1992)*
Director: Tom DiCillo
Character: Johnny Suede

Cool World *(1992)*
Director: Ralph Bakshi
Character: Frank Harris

A River Runs Through It *(1992)*
Director: Robert Redford
Character: Paul Maclean

Kalifornia *(1993)*
Director: Dominic Sena
Character: Early Grayce

True Romance *(1993)*
Director: Tony Scott
Character: Floyd

The Favor *(1994)*
Director: Donald Petrie
Character: Elliott

Interview With the Vampire *(1994)*
Director: Neil Jordan
Character: Louis

Legends of the Fall *(1994)*
Director: Edward Zwick
Character: Tristan Ludlow

Seven *(1995)*
Director: David Fincher
Character: David Mills

12 Monkeys *(1995)*
Director: Terry Gilliam
Character: Jeffrey Goines

Sleepers *(1996)*
Director: Barry Levinson
Character: Michael Sullivan

The Devil's Own *(1997)*
Director: Alan J. Pakula
Character: Frankie "the Angel"
McGuire

Seven Years in Tibet *(1997)*
Director: Jean-Jacques Annaud
Character: Heinrich Harrer

Contributors

LORRAINE ALI is a senior critic at *Rolling Stone,* and has also written for *US,* the *New York Times, Details, Entertainment Weekly, Spin* and *Mademoiselle.* She contributed to Rolling Stone Press's *Cobain* and *The Rolling Stone Book of Women in Rock: Trouble Girls.*

LAWRENCE FRASCELLA is a New York–based freelance writer who is still writing film reviews. He just completed a novel, *The Family Medium.*

CHRIS MUNDY is a former senior writer and current contributing editor at *Rolling Stone* and *US.* He wrote the introduction to *Rolling Stone's Alt-Rock-a-Rama,* and his writing also appears in the Rolling Stone Press books *Cobain* and *The Rolling Stone Film Reader.* He is now at work on his first novel.

BARBARA O'DAIR is the editor of *US.* Formerly the deputy music editor of *Rolling Stone,* she has also worked as a senior editor at *Entertainment Weekly* and the *Village Voice.* She has written for *Rolling Stone, Spin,* the *Village Voice* and other publications. She contributed the Introduction to *Madonna: The Rolling Stone Files* and is the editor of *The Rolling Stone Book of Women in Rock: Trouble Girls.*

MARK SELIGER is the chief photographer at *Rolling Stone* and *US.*

PETER TRAVERS has been *Rolling Stone's* film critic and senior features editor for film since 1989. He was a former chair of the New York Film Critics Circle and was the film and theater critic for *People.* Currently a regular film commentator for CNN, Travers also edited *The Rolling Stone Film Reader.*

PICTURE CREDITS All photographs by Mark Seliger except the following: Barry Blitt, 123 • Stephen Brodner, 126 • Everett Collection, 136 (1–7), 137 (8, 9) • Hungry Dog Studios, 135 • Laura Levine, 131 • Photofest, 137 (10–13) • Seth Poppel Yearbook Archives, 11

Acknowledgments

The difficulty pinning down Brad Pitt that Chris Mundy so eloquently describes in his highly entertaining and insightful introduction is kind of like what we went through creating *Brad Pitt,* the book. In fact, if it hadn't been for a team of motivated, determined individuals, this volume would not exist: designer Richard Baker, Chris Mundy, Rolling Stone Press associate editor Shawn Dahl and editorial assistant Ann Abel, film critic Peter Travers, photo editor Fiona McDonagh, *US* editor Barbara O'Dair, Wenner Media creative director Fred Woodward, writer Lorraine Ali, Little, Brown's Michael Pietsch and Paul Harrington, and our literary agent Sarah Lazin. Many thanks to *US* and *Rolling Stone's* Jann S. Wenner, Kent Brownridge, John Lagana, Tom Worley, Chris Raymond, Gary Randazzo, Alvin Ling, Maury Viola, Janice Borowicz and Lucy Elghazoly, as well as Little, Brown's Teresa Lo Conte, Susan Canavan, Nora Krug and David Gibbs. Other invaluable contributors to our project include photographer Mark Seliger; artists Hungry Dog Studio, Laura Levine, Barry Blitt and Steve Brodner; and Lawrence Frascella, Jancee Dunn, Margy Rochlin, Jeff Giles, Holly Millea, Peter Kenis, Patricia Romanowski, Will Rigby, Gina Zucker, Stephanie Chernikowski, Elsie St. Léger, Susan Richardson, Laura Sandlin, Yoomi Chong, Jennifer Chun, Bess Wong, Samantha Schwartz, Chris Bishop, Mark Markheim Laboratory, Cindy Guagenti and Betty Raymond. And to the charismatic and elusive Brad Pitt, thanks for making our project so challenging.

HOLLY GEORGE-WARREN, editor

ROLLING STONE PRESS

MAY 1997